BRITISH RAILWAYS

PAST and PRESENT

No 55

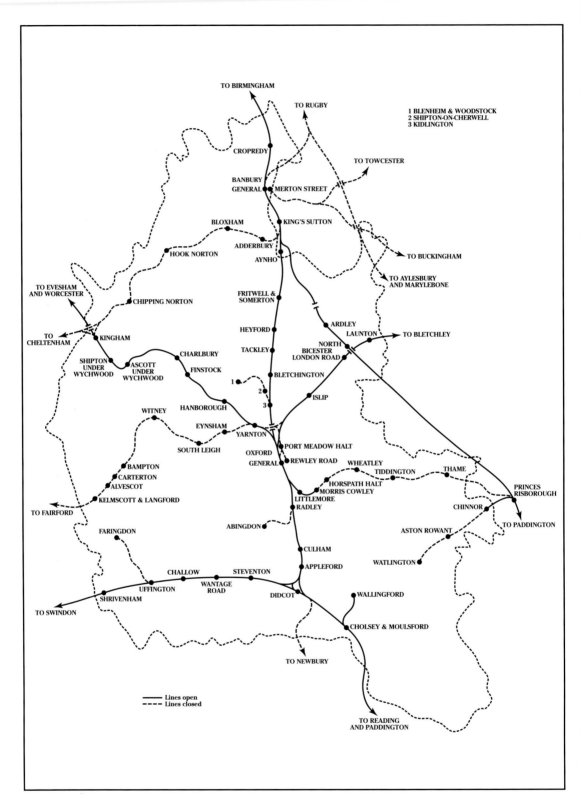

Map of the area covered by this book, showing locations featured or referred to in the text.

BRITISH RAILWAYS

PAST and PRESENT

No 55

Oxfordshire
A second selection

John Stretton

Past and Present

Past & Present Publishing Ltd

First published in 2006

British Library Cataloguing in Publication Data

A catalogue record for this book is available from the British Library.

ISBN 1 85895 203 4
ISBN 978 1 85895 203 1

Past & Present Publishing Ltd
The Trundle
Ringstead Road
Great Addington
Kettering
Northants NN14 4BW

Tel/Fax: 01536 330588
email: sales@nostalgiacollection.com
Website: www.nostalgiacollection.com

Printed and bound in Great Britain

ACKNOWLEDGEMENTS

As with any project such as this, there are highs and lows. The latter usually come when you arrive at a promising location to find that the promise is frustrated and/or unfulfilled. The former, however, are more likely to derive from the material sent by the various contributors. Almost without exception there are gems and the unexpected, and the arrival of each package was a source of anticipation and delight. For around 120 'past' photographic spaces I had in excess of 700 prints – and that is ignoring colour slides that I knew were available! Again, as with others books that I have prepared, the project would have been so much weaker without these ready and helpful supporters, especially those who have lent me their precious negatives, to provide best-quality images. Thus, without further hesitation, I thank all who have helped me, no matter how small the assistance. It has all been worth it, but there those who deserve especial mention.

I must first thank John Edgington, not just for his courtesy, swift responses and his phenomenal and widespread knowledge, but also for his own contributions and his proof-reading. In no particular order, the following also deserve truly grateful thanks for their help and support: Frank Cassell and Mike Mitchell, specifically, for loaning me their excellent negatives to produce the magnificent pictures seen herein; Mike Esau, for help with his own and John Spencer Gilks's photographs; Richard Casserley – as always! – for his co-operation and patience; Peter Treloar, for dipping into his massive collection; Roger Carpenter and the Lens of Sutton Collection; and the rest of the photographers who are credited where appropriate.

Everyone at Silver Link has played their part in the production; as has my wife, Judi, who again has borne with the loss of me to a computer and hundreds of photographs strewn across the floor! Without them all, this book would not have seen the light of day. Thank you, each and every one!

CONTENTS

CHACOMBE ROAD HALT: In the heyday of railway building there appeared to have been greater emphasis on architectural style than cutting costs, even when the terrain was not immediately suitable to the required construction. Even such out-of-the-way places as tiny rural communities benefited from this approach, as can be seen in this delightful study of Chacombe Road Halt signal box and station approach. Seen on 5 April 1959, this view from ground level could almost be from any period in the previous hundred years, even down to the rudimentary lamp to illuminate the footpath! *John Spencer Gilks*

Above FARINGDON: Architectural style was also to the fore on 'God's Wonderful Railway', as was the presence of many engaging rural branch lines. A superb example of the latter was the short stretch from Uffington to the town of Faringdon, seen here on 26 April 1959 as diminutive No 1365 waits to begin the Herculean task of heading the 4.00pm non-stop Rail Enthusiasts' Club special to Challow! Passenger services to this terminus were an early casualty of railway economics, ending on the last day of 1951; consequently, the sight of a loco and coaches in the platform is one of great excitement for the local children! Freight continued until 1 July 1963, hence the well-preserved infrastructure on site. Note the distinctive 'mushroom' station building. *John Spencer Gilks*

Left UFFINGTON: The other end of the branch sees a highly unusual sight on 3 August 1975. Captured from the 1897 roadbridge over the station site by one of the travelling engineers, the prototype APT-E is stabled in the up loop while much discussion and some refreshment is taken during main-line testing over the GWR main line west of Reading. Note the remains of the goods platform on the right – this was swept away some 20 years later when the site was used to manufacture track panels to be installed locally. Immediately to the left of the train, the up main line looks to have been recently reballasted. *Alan Rimmer*

INTRODUCTION

In steam days Oxford was a very special place for railway enthusiasts. In company with very few similar locations throughout the UK, it was a place where representatives of all four major pre-Grouping railways and, later, BR regions could be seen daily. Being a main GWR artery between London, Birmingham and Birkenhead – served by a medium-sized but busy engine shed at Oxford – locos from 'God's Wonderful Railway' abounded in all shapes and sizes, but an equally healthy variety of motive power also came from the Southern Railway/Region, LMS/Midland Region and LNER/Eastern Region. Many of these visitors came off their trains on reaching the city, creating yet more interest for the spotter and general public alike. Elsewhere in the county, places like Banbury, Bicester and Kingham had their own share of interest and appeal and – post-1974, the period covered in this book – the county boundary changes brought the GWR main line between Shrivenham and Cholsey into focus.

Being a second selection of 'then and now' views of the county, this volume has given me the opportunity of trawling for fresh shots, and I have been fortunate to come up with many that, as far as I am aware, have not been seen in print before. It has been a joy and an occasional frustration visiting the 'old haunts' – in some cases it took serious detective work to discover and identify the footprints of the original photographers, and the passage of time has meant that in some cases the current view is either meaningless or is little different from that seen in the earlier volume. As a result, I have eschewed repeats of the proverbial brick wall and in some places have referred the reader to that earlier collection – I trust that I will be forgiven! Similarly, some of the history of the county's lines is also given in the first book, and I have not repeated it here, except in the form of expanded captions where appropriate.

As with other titles in this series, there are occasions when the railway has all but disappeared from the scene, but happily there is still much to be seen on today's system within Oxfordshire's boundary, and there are also areas where remnants of the past are still extant, including such as Hook Norton Tunnel, which has been put to good modern use. Viewing all this variety has been part of the delight of the preparation of this volume and I hope that the disparate images will give satisfaction. In addition, I have broken the strict 'past and present' format to include illustrations that deserved to be seen on their own merits, and I crave indulgence for this personal preference.

An example of the kind of inter-company/regional cross-country services that made Oxford such an attractive place for spotters and enthusiasts in earlier years. Here is a 1907 GCR handbill for excursions to various destinations beyond that company's network.

Steam disappeared under normal circumstances from the county over the first half-dozen years of the 1960s, but far-sighted cameramen had already recorded much that was around prior to this, which now gives us both pleasure and a hankering for days gone by. Sadly, our present railway is much poorer in aesthetics, especially where infrastructure and signalling are concerned, but with the proliferation of liveries and new types of motive power since Privatisation in 1994, there is at least some variety still to be had. The railway may be much changed, but for the photographer there is much to capture, and the challenge, without steam, to create a satisfying image is now even greater than of yore! Happily, Oxford, Didcot, Banbury and Bicester are still major players within the county – each with its individual character – and long may it remain so. It would be nice to see some stations and/or lines re-open, but while it is probably wishful thinking in most instances, one can but dream! And there is still constant change. First Great Western's 'Adelantes' are the latest arrivals, on the service to Worcester, but it does not seem many months since Virgin's 'Voyagers' or Thames's 'Turbos' were new, or since Oxford station still had an underpass and the depot serviced locomotives and DMUs. There is a message there for present-day photographers – the future will need the images that you could take today!

GWR main line south through Banbury

CROPREDY is the most northerly point in the county, just a couple of miles south of the border with Warwickshire. Although a wayside station, it was graced with three important sidings, for local ironstone and aluminium industries, amongst others. Some of the extensive infrastructure can be judged from this view of No 6980 *Llanrumney Hall* approaching the station from the north on Saturday 5 September 1964, with what looks to be a rake of Southern green coaches. As the regular York-Bournemouth cross-country trains joined this ex-GWR main line south of Cropredy, it would be interesting to know the nature of this working – possibly a train from Birkenhead to Bournemouth, or to Dover, Hastings and Ramsgate. Note that the 'Hall' is devoid of both nameplates and shedplate. Nominally an Oxley engine at this date, it was transferred to Banbury seven weeks later, from where it was withdrawn on 9 October 1965.

As with so many other parts of our railway system, the transformation over the years is dramatic. In this view from 31 July 2005, only the signal – now a colour light, but roughly in the same position as the tall semaphore above – the two remaining main-line tracks and the road overbridge, just visible in the far distance, are common to the two views. No 221119 *Amelia Earhart*, one of Virgin's tilting 'Voyagers', represents the modern 'express'. Though not readily apparent in this view, the tell-tale signs of the old station and the down siding, to the left of the 'Hall' above, are identifiable on the ground. *Bryan Hicks/MJS*

BANBURY: Over the past 50 years Banbury station has seen major extension and re-organisation, in both the number of platform faces and the shape and size of the entrance buildings. As seen in 1953, the design and the extensive use of wood harks back to an earlier age and was rapidly becoming a real constraint on expansion and customer service. A photographer stands for his portrait, alongside two delightful period cars.

The rebuilding of the station – almost futuristic for its time – was completed in the last years of the 1950s, and it lasted for the next half century. More recently, a rethink for the entrance has led to cosmetic changes, with a far more light and airy access. On 9 July 2005 another visitor pauses in roughly the position of the photographer above. The road overbridge at the northern end of the station, faintly visible in the 1953 view, is again just in view between the glass wall and the lamp standard. *MJS collection/MJS*

BANBURY: Having gained access to the platforms, the photographer has captured an express arriving at the station from the north. On an unidentified date during the spring of 1955, No 6011 *King James I* slows for the station stop with an up express, probably a Birkenhead-Paddington service. Notice that the 'King' still sports a single chimney at this date; the fitting of a double blastpipe did not come until March 1956. Built at Swindon in April 1928, it spent much of its working life operating from Wolverhampton (Stafford Road) shed. A move south to Old Oak Common came on 6 October 1962, just four short months before withdrawal on the following 9 February. Note the Eastern Region coach to the right of the 'King', from a local from Woodford Halse on the ex-GCR route, and awaiting return.

Fifty years on, much has changed, but much still remains identifiable. On 9 July 2005 Virgin 'Voyager' No 220017 *Bombardier Voyager*, just short of four years old, represents modern long-distance diesel traction as it enters the station with the 1V60 Virgin Trains 1333 Birmingham (New Street)-Reading service. The sidings to the right are no longer crammed with wagons and are succumbing to a grassy invasion, the buildings beyond have replaced the house and hoarding seen above, the semaphore signal at the end of the down platform has been replaced by colour lights, but the signal box, seen beyond the road bridge, is still in situ, and some semaphores do survive, to control exit from the extreme left-hand platform face. *Alec Ford/MJS*

BANBURY is seen again before the late-1950s alterations. Looking south from the northern end of the down main platform on 27 October 1956, a train stands ready on the right for a local trip, while on the left the sidings are being shunted.

In the comparative view on 9 July 2005 the late-1950s edifice is virtually unchanged since new, apart from the station name on the external wall, but despite the structure being much enhanced and enlarged over the earlier one, the view still gives a much cleaner and open impression. One of Chiltern Railways' front-line 'Turbo' units, No 168111, stands ready on the right to restart its journey to Birmingham. *H. C. Casserley/MJS*

BANBURY: As seen from the old A422 road, bringing traffic from Middleton Cheney into the centre of Banbury, the station – then known as 'General' – is here 'brand new', with the original external lettering. On 6 August 1960 an empty Pressed Steel three-car WR DMU passes the lower-quadrant semaphore signal on its way to the holding sidings on the other side of the road bridge, having discharged its load of passengers from the 4.18pm service from Paddington. Just beyond, No 6931 *Aldborough Hall* waits in the bay for its turn to haul a northbound local train.

Instantly recognisable as the same place, there has been much change but also many things that have survived the passage of 45 years to 9 July 2005. Not least, of course, is the station building, but thankfully the trackwork is virtually untouched and even the kink in the foreground railing is still there! Elsewhere, barriers have been added to the short platform on the right to allow for car parking; modern lights and station nameboards have replaced previous styles; and two platform semaphores and the water column have gone, although one arm is still in use. The greatest change is the new Royal Mail facility dominating the left horizon. *Michael Mensing/MJS*

BANBURY: With the engine shed and gas-holder nearby, the southerly view from the station at Banbury had more inherent interest than that facing north. No 7924 *Thornycroft Hall* approaches the platform on 31 July 1965 with a Bournemouth-York cross-country train. So late in the day for steam on ex-GWR metals – and with a handmade front numberplate and stripped of nameplates and brackets – it is likely that the 'Hall' was deputising for a failed English Electric Class 3 diesel, which would normally be working these trains in this period. Items of interest include the signal box, a plethora of semaphore signals, the rather strangely placed trackside clock, the diminutive building with the tall chimney, and sidings left and right.

Ten years later diesels hold sway on all services, but many items from the earlier scene survive, with only the new building beyond the semaphore gantry on the left to show any progress. No 47326 speeds towards the station with an empty 'merry-go-round' coal train heading north, having discharged its load at Didcot. Named *Saltley Depot Quality Assured* at that depot on 9 December 1994, this honour was only to last some four years!

Yet another tilting 'Voyager' is handling the top-link cross-country services through Banbury. On 9 July 2005 No 221143 *Auguste Picard* slows for the station stop, forming the delayed 1S71 Virgin 1305 Reading-Glasgow Central service. This time much has been swept away over the ensuing 30 years, but incredibly a semaphore survives, though a replacement for earlier ones, and the signal box is still in place. Electric cable trunking has appeared in the foreground, and to the left new sidings have been recently put in place. *Frank Cassell/Tom Heavyside/ MJS*

BANBURY SHED: In common with hundreds of other engine sheds throughout the country in the period when steam ruled the rails, Banbury was a haven for healthy numbers of locomotives and a Mecca for enthusiasts, especially at the weekends. One element that added variety and bonus for this location, however, was the passage of cross-country services such as the York-Bournemouth, bringing 'foreign' visitors to this GWR stronghold. While many engine changes took place at Oxford, Banbury was also used, and one such guest, seen here, is LNER Ivatt 'Atlantic' No 4434. In this photograph, taken on 29 March 1936, it waits to return home, standing in company with No 4361 and a phalanx of other GWR types.

On 31 May 1966, just four months from closure, the same shed is now temporary shelter to far fewer locos and of differing types. Right to left are Nos 7029 *Clun Castle*, 92138 and 48726, with the latter two coaled and ready to go; respectively, the pair were to see the end of their working lives at Speke Junction in June 1967 and Banbury in September 1966. *Clun Castle* was withdrawn from Worcester five months prior to this view, at the very end of 1965, and is here awaiting its future fate.

Clun Castle is again seen on Banbury shed in the third view, this time in 1965, before withdrawal and in receipt of some attention. Note that the loco is already without front number and nameplates. To the left, ex-Crosti-boilered No 92029 is also without front number, but is still in active service. The end for this engine came at Birkenhead in November 1967. *Les Hanson, Peter Treloar collection/Roger Carpenter/ MJS collection*

BANBURY MERTON STREET: At its height Banbury was graced with two stations, that in Merton Street, adjacent to the GWR site, being the terminus for the very rural ex-LNWR branch from Verney Junction via Buckingham and an ex-S&MJR leg from Towcester. Despite its relatively small size, with just two, largely wooden platforms, it initially had a full range of facilities, even down to the ability to handle livestock, horse boxes and 'carriages and motor cars by passenger train'! It also had a 5-ton crane. The branch from Towcester was an early casualty, with passenger services withdrawn on 2 July 1951. Traffic between Buckingham and Merton Street ended on 2 January 1961 (passengers) and 2 December 1963 (freight), and the end came on 6 June 1966, when the short spur from General station, through 'Banbury Junction' to an exchange siding, was closed. In this view from the late 1950s – the car was registered between June and October 1958 – all the post-1951 facilities are still in use, with freight wagons by the goods shed.

By 9 July 2005, nearly 40 years after final closure, the road layout is still recognisable, as is the now much greener 'embankment' on the left, but elsewhere all is changed. New building has appeared to the right, together with a post-box, and there is work in hand on the old station site to build 130 one- and two-bedroom apartments. The construction site does not have the same aesthetic qualities of the old station! *Roger Carpenter/MJS*

Above BANBURY MERTON STREET: As seen opposite, the old station was under development in 2005, with fencing preventing intrepid photographers from accessing it! We therefore look on this page at two views inside the station in happier times. In an undated view – probably from the later years of the 1950s and still with the 'hawk's-eye' running-in board – the by then regulation single-car DMU stands at the eastern platform face, waiting to make the relatively short run to Buckingham. Note the mainly wooden platform, with one patch of stone immediately before the attractively shaped trainshed, which had lost its glazing many years previously. Note the healthy amount of freight, evidenced by the number of wagons right and left. The houses in the distance face the A422 road, mentioned on page 13. *MJS collection*

Below Moving closer into the station proper, we have a delightful scene as a railman prepares to check the ticket of one of the travellers. Note the steps up to the carriage from the low platform, the station name boldly ignoring the fact that there was an alternative station in the town and the parcels barrow awaiting trade. This view on 31 December 1960 is poignant, as it is the very last day of public passenger services to Buckingham. *Edwin Wilmshurst*

FRITWELL & SOMERTON: Almost immediately on leaving Banbury General station, the railway ran into Northamptonshire and continued in that county until just south of King's Sutton station. The first station back in Oxfordshire was Fritwell & Somerton, representing two villages on the northern edge of the Upper Heyford Airfield. Both communities were again rural and isolated, with Somerton being the closer of the two, although the halt only announced that location until 1907, so as not to clash with Somerton in Somerset. Able to handle livestock and horse boxes, as well as general freight and passenger traffic, the station also operated a 1ton 10cwt crane. Peak traffic was during the First World War, with a progressive decline thereafter until closure in 1964, on 4 May for passengers and 2 November for freight. This view, from the early years of the 20th century, looking north, shows a well kept station garden, the signal box beyond the down platform and, to its right, the cattle dock with its white-painted pen.

From a train it would be impossible to identify that a station had ever existed here, and even on the ground it is hard to believe, such has been the reclamation by tree growth over the last 40 years. This is the same view on 17 July 2005, with only the ancient-looking fencing on the extreme right, at the top of an approach incline, giving any clue. Note the potential invitation to vandalism, with the two concrete sleepers dumped close to rails on which trains could be travelling at anything up to 125mph! *R. M. Casserley collection/MJS*

HEYFORD station, situated just a handful of miles south-west of the airfield, was actually next to the hamlet of Lower Heyford, cheek-by-jowl with both the Oxford Canal and the River Cherwell. Originally a broad gauge single track, the line opened on 2 September 1850 and became mixed gauge and double track from 1 October 1852. It was converted to standard gauge in the latter years of the 19th century and this accounts for the wider than usual spacing between the platforms, as seen here looking north on 6 July 1958, with the station enjoying a brief quiet time between the many services along this north-south 'main line'. With the main buildings virtually identical to those a few miles north at Aynho, there was ample provision for the travelling public and staff alike. The 22-lever signal box, lower left, sat on the down platform, and operated until September 1968.

The slightly wider angle of the 17 July 2005 view allows us to see just how close the canal is to the railway here, a factor hidden by the up station building above. Despite now having a new, more substantial footbridge – installed early in 2005 at a cost of £½million, to replace the 1911-built GWR one that had been weakened by corrosion – the rest of the public facilities, provided in 2005 by First Great Western Link, are sparse and minimalist compared to former years, with just rudimentary shelters. A Thames 'Turbo' 165/1 unit restarts from its brief pause at the station and runs south under the east-west minor road, from the bridge carrying which both photographs were taken. *H. C. Casserley/MJS*

HEYFORD: The low, summer-evening sun adds to the delightfully rural and picturesque scene, as an unidentified ex-GWR '4300' Class 2-6-0 locomotive, with a Hawksworth high-sided tender, heads south through the station with a through freight, adorned with a suitable Class H lamp headcode. The canal lies empty and placid, and the single station siding, centre left, is equally untroubled with traffic.

The first thing that strikes in this view from 17 July 2005 is how much has been hidden and/or transformed by the growth of greenery over the past 50 years or so. The down siding has gone and its course is now completely masked by the line of trees on the left. The canal boundary wall is also hidden by bushy growth, while the canalside fields and dwellings are all interspersed with expanding numbers and heights of trees. 'Turbo' No 165128 slows for the station stop, operating as a Banbury-Oxford/Reading local service. *MJS collection/MJS*

TACKLEY: Unlike the other stations already seen on this main-line stretch, Tackley was a 'Johnnie-come-lately', only being opened on 6 April 1931. Initially called Tackley Halt, as seen here on 24 August 1963, the word 'Halt' was officially dropped from 5 March 1961, but the 'new' sign, placed on the platform end in the late 1950s to replace the previous one with raised lettering, still carries the old name. Having taken over the train at Banbury, No 5026 *Criccieth Castle* rushes southwards with a Bradford Exchange-Poole cross-country summer holiday service, with the appropriate four-character reporting number chalked on the smokebox door. Note the 'cheap' nature of the station, which enjoyed only a short platform length.

Though serving a somewhat limited catchment area, the station has survived and has been lengthened to accommodate the requirements of current Health & Safety considerations. Tree growth has again altered the aesthetics and ambience of the station, giving a much more hemmed-in, 'corridor' feel than the previously open aspect. On 17 July 2005 No 220024 *Sheffield Voyager*, approaching its fourth birthday, plays the part of the 'Castle' above, as it operates its own version of a cross-country train, though of much shorter length! *John Spencer Gilks/MJS*

King's Sutton to Kingham

ADDERBURY: As the line south of Banbury re-entered Oxfordshire, south of King's Sutton, a branch struck west to head for Kingham, and the first station was Adderbury, seen here in the very early 1970s, some time after its closure and after the last freight train had trundled along the branch. To the right is the old Station Master's house. Losing its passenger services on 4 June 1951, withdrawal of freight facilities westwards to Hook Norton came on 4 November 1963, leaving the short stub from King's Sutton, which served local merchants until 18 August 1969. Though here abandoned, the station nameboard and waiting shelters remain, as does the starter semaphore, all awaiting reclamation.

On 9 July 2005 the only recognisable sign that this is the same view is the old Station Master's house on the right. Although the house is virtually unchanged, its garden and the rest of the railway infrastructure have received dramatic attention. With the railway gone, the bridge carrying the main Oxford-Banbury A423 road (now the A4260 since the opening of the M40!) was infilled to road level and the old garden extended, with the necessary earth coming from the construction site of a new Sainsbury's supermarket in Banbury! The vehicles just visible through the trees, left of centre, stand on the alignment of the old trackbed. *MJS collection/MJS*

ADDERBURY: Following withdrawal of freight traffic on 18 August 1969, there was still the occasional trip working to salvage various items. The last of these ran on 3 October 1969, and an unidentified Class 47 stands in the platform waiting for the run back to the main line. Some idea of the importance of this location can be judged from the size of the signal box and the sidings on both sides of the through lines.

The same view on 9 July 2005 shows the alignment of the old through lines running from the telegraph pole, centre right, to the left of the picture, alongside the greenery on the far side of the yard. The two sole surviving artefacts of the railway on this day were part of the old goods shed – behind the photographer – and the drainage culvert that has prevented development of this lower part of the industrial site. The southern parapet of this latter is hidden by what appears to be bushes to the left of the end wall of the units. *MJS collection/MJS*

BLOXHAM was the next stop, and looking towards Chipping Norton this was the view as seen from the A361 roadbridge in April 1957, two months short of six years since passenger services were dispensed with between Banbury and Chipping Norton, on 4 June 1951. Freight struggled on until final withdrawal on 4 November 1963. Note the station garden still tidily maintained, as it had been throughout the 20th century, and how the trees, barely waist height in the early 1900s (see *British Railways Past and Present No 15*, p129), are now dominating the mid-scene. A gateway has been added to the entrance road compared to earlier views, but otherwise the scene is little changed from 60 years earlier.

Yes, this is the same view! Incredible as it may seem, this is the same vantage point from the A361 on 9 July 2005. Slightly more meaningful comparative shots can be found in the earlier Oxfordshire volume referred to above, before these latest houses were built. To the left of the scene is a park, from which the course of the old railway alignment can be judged by the subsequent housing developments on a higher level to the green open space. *Mike Mitchell/MJS*

Top HOOK NORTON: In common with other stations on this branch within the county boundary, Hook Norton had a short platform, befitting the relatively limited size of the nearby village and the very rural nature of the surrounding countryside. However, there were some half-dozen ironstone quarries locally, served by industrial lines, and over the years these contributed greatly to the level of traffic seen here. Local passenger trains were short and latterly of the push-pull variety with one coach; W83 was a well-used example in the years before closure. Certainly the length of train seen here would not normally have been seen. On 14 September 1963 No 6111 runs round its train while visiting with an REC enthusiasts' railtour. In 2005 the site is a private industrial unit and permission for photographs was refused. An earlier comparison can again be seen in *British Railways Past & Present No 15. John Spencer Gilks*

Middle and bottom HOOK NORTON: Very shortly after leaving the station the railway turned southwards for a time, crossed two viaducts, then, a mile after the halt, ran through a 418-yard tunnel. Looking towards Chipping Norton in the early 1950s, No 5391 leaves the northern portal with a Class J freight – possibly with an incorrect headcode – demonstrating the varied needs of the area. Note the very neat and tidy trackbed, stone retaining walls and the attractive grass and drainage channel design above the tunnel mouth.

On 9 July 2005 the northern portal was inaccessible, so this is a comparative view at the south end, now a nature reserve. The retaining walls still remain, but have deteriorated and partly crumbled over the years, partly obstructing the old trackbed, along with progressive floral inhabitation. The tunnel is now blocked from public access, to act as a bat roost, and the entrance is among the greenery seen just to the left of the sign on the right-hand embankment. *Peter Treloar collection/MJS*

CHIPPING NORTON was the next location of any size on the branch within the county, and some of its inherent importance locally was recognised when the line was threatened with withdrawal of passenger services so soon after Nationalisation. While the stretch westwards from the junction at King's Sutton – arguably the most strategic part, taking villagers into the local centre at Banbury – had the axe applied on 4 June 1951, Chipping Norton remained open for the route to Kingham and on to Cheltenham. However, this link with the outside world was withdrawn on 3 December 1962, with freight, and therefore the whole of this branch within the county, succumbing on 7 September 1964. Two years earlier, looking towards Kingham in the autumn of 1962, freight services are evident from the wagons in the distant yard and within the goods shed, and the signal box still operates for the last two months of passenger trade.

Although the bridge under the A44, through which the line entered the station, has been infilled, this comparative view is still available from the roadside, albeit now somewhat restricted by progressive bush and tree growth. The linking points are the tree just beyond the far unit in the builder's yard and the evergreen to the right. *Joe Moss, Roger Carpenter collection/MJS*

CHIPPING NORTON: This is the view of the main station building – seen from the platform side on the opposite page – viewed from the approach road off the A44. Again seen in the autumn of 1962, with just two months of passenger services left, the posters exhort 'Holidays in Britain' and 'Holiday Camping Coaches' – surely a little late in the season for these! – and announce the imminent demise of passenger traffic. There also seems to have been a removal of the canopy over the Booking Hall entrance. Note the semi-permanent Nissen hut, the church in the distance, and the rear of the signal box.

The approach road still remains, serving now to bring customers to an industrial site. As seen on 14 July 2005 the station site has been totally redeveloped, with current occupant Travis Perkins housing their 'Timber & Building Supplies' across the old trackbed, at 90 degrees to the old station building. *Joe Moss, Roger Carpenter collection/MJS*

KINGHAM: Although a relatively small village, with only 816 inhabitants in 1901, Kingham boasted a sizeable and busy station and even a locomotive shed! The reason was its location on the main Oxford-Evesham/Worcester route and as a terminus for branches from Banbury and Cheltenham. Looking north towards Evesham, the left-hand tracks, serving Platforms 1 and 2, form the through route, with the branch platforms, which effectively formed a long loop, standing to the right. In 1962, in the last months of its operation, a Chipping Norton-bound train waits in Platform 3, with parcels items about to be loaded into the last coach, so departure is not imminent. Services to Chipping Norton ceased on 3 December 1962. The bridge in the distance formed a link between the two branches, enabling freight trains – and one 'Ports to Ports' express between May 1906 and September 1939 – to run direct between Banbury and Cheltenham without entering Kingham station.

Following total closure of both branch routes from 7 September 1964, Platforms 3 and 4 were abandoned, the tracks ripped up (in July 1966) and all infrastructure, including the linking footbridge, removed. Nature has since progressively taken control and, more recently, the space beneath the B4450 roadbridge that allowed the loop to run past the station, has been infilled and the bridge parapet rebuilt. This was the view on 14 July 2005, with the present station devoid of the previous 'furniture'. *MJS collection/MJS*

KINGHAM was originally called Chipping Norton Junction when it opened on 10 August 1855, but gained the name of its nearby village from 1 May 1909; however, the link to Chipping Norton – and to Bourton-on-the-Water in the opposite direction – is not forgotten, being enshrined in the large station nameboard. This undated view, probably from around 1960, shows that local services are still running, a 'totem' station sign is affixed to the nearby lamp standard, and the overall roof has been removed from the footbridge, but an attempt has been made at smartening the place with white paint on the remaining parts of the footbridge as well as station canopy and railings.

The comparative view on a dull and damp 27 October 1989 shows a denuded station, with a perfunctory waiting shelter and little to encourage the intending traveller. Note the 'new' station sign – the old one repainted and now without the 'Change for...' appendage – the ¾ milepost adjacent to it, and the former branch platforms still visible.

By 14 July 2005 the untidy branch platforms have been hidden by subsequent growth, softening the bare effect, and the general demeanour of the station has been improved by new platform surfaces and a lick of bright blue paint, while posters and hanging baskets adorn the waiting shelter. The car park, on the right, has also been smartened. Note the survival of both station sign and milepost. The new roadbridge parapet, mentioned opposite, can just be seen beyond the footbridge, to the left of the open platforms. Celebrations were held during August 2005 to celebrate the 150th anniversary of opening. *MJS collection/MJS (2)*

KINGHAM: Looking in the opposite direction from the previous view, we are again looking north, with the freight avoiding line on the bridge beyond the signal box. To the right of the latter is the single-road engine shed, occupied by what looks to be a Dean 0-6-0. To the right of the substantial water tower a gang of workers are attending to the track leading off to the right towards Chipping Norton – notice the lack of 'hi-vis' vests and hard hats in those far-off halcyon days! In this view, around 1953, some idea of the amount of goods traffic handled here can be judged from the occupied sidings both to the left and beyond the overbridge.

It is hard to imagine that there were once extra platforms here, or branch lines, sidings, engine shed, etc. With the abandonment of previous infrastructure, apart from the recent refurbishment of the station car park on the left, nature has gladly reclaimed the land, leaving just the through route intact, although even this was threatened with closure during the past 20 years or so. A sunny 14 July 2005, together with fresh paintwork on lamps and tidy platforms, makes for a pleasing scene, despite the knowledge of what was there once upon a time! *Joe Moss, Roger Carpenter collection/MJS*

Kingham to Handborough

SHIPTON UNDER WYCHWOOD is the first station reached when heading south-east from Kingham, on the 'main line' to Oxford. Seen in this view around 1910, it boasted around a dozen staff and served around 700 inhabitants of the nearby village, as well as being a link to what was to become the tourist 'honeypot' of Burford; indeed, at one point its nameboard heralded 'Shipton for Burford'. As a train leaves for Kingham, the 1884 signal box will reset the signals. Elsewhere, the horse from the nearby wagon casually munches on grass, and on the left is the weighbridge of the impressive flour mill.

On 24 July 2005 the massive building still stands, operating as base for F. W. P. Matthews Ltd, 'The Cotswold Flour Millers', and the station is still open, with a limited number of trains calling daily, but elsewhere all is changed. The substantial goods shed, seen centre right in the 'past' view, is no more and the sidings have all been torn up. The access road and flat ground level area are still there, but now the exclusive preserve of the mill. Main services over this route were turned over to First Great Western's 'Adelante' Class 180s earlier in 2005 and one is seen here heading straight through the station, operating as the 1D43 1548 Paddington-Hereford service. *Lens of Sutton collection/MJS*

ASCOTT UNDER WYCHWOOD: The Wychwood Forest, stretching from west of Shipton through to Charlbury, is again commemorated on the station sign here, just a couple of miles or so east of Shipton. More typical of a wayside station than its near neighbour, Ascott did have a goods siding until September 1965, but no crane or other handling facilities. In this view towards Oxford on 18 July 1959, both platforms are still in use, the turnout to the siding can be seen at the end of the right-hand platform and, just beyond, is a crossover to assist with freight workings.

As can be seen, almost exactly 46 years later provision of facilities both on and off the station has been reduced dramatically. The previous up track had been lifted by the early 1970s, but its platform was still extant – complete with station nameboard and waiting shelter – in 1972! The siding remained in use until the mid-1980s, but the remaining station was becoming a sorry sight. Happily, although all evidence of the up platform has been swept away, the area has received some 'TLC' and, in this view from 14 July 2005, the station itself now boasts the same smart blue livery already observed at Kingham. *H. C. Casserley/MJS*

CHARLBURY: Originally opened with very short platforms, the down side at Charlbury, on which the photographer is standing, was lengthened in 1928. The up platform, however, was somewhat hampered by the siding to the coal wharf, which had itself been extended in 1885 and the turnout to which can just be seen bottom left in this view from 18 July 1959. With a typical Brunel chalet-style station building gracing the up platform, the station also enjoyed the facilities of a goods shed – until late 1970 – a 30cwt crane and a 34-lever signal box. This latter, however, was lost with the singling of the line through the station on 29 November 1971.

Although the coal wharf was removed many years ago, the sole remaining platform was not initially lengthened as, with three-car DMUs handling most of the passenger traffic, the existing length was acceptable. However, with the increase in the number of HSTs on the route and their stopping at the station, safety considerations dictated that some action be taken and the present longer platform can be judged from this 14 July 2005 view, when compared to that above. Also, it is pleasing to report that heritage considerations have also been fully appreciated, with Brunel's building and the original station nameboard – and even ex-GWR seats – all being retained and refurbished. With the booking office still manned at times, the general ambience leads to a much happier experience for the travelling public. *H. C. Casserley/MJS*

FINSTOCK was typical of so many GWR wayside halts, with the most rudimentary of passenger facilities and little in the way of protection from the elements, especially as it was some distance from the tiny hamlet that it served. Only opened in 1934, the platforms were not to see hoards of passengers, as the village only enjoyed some 450-470 inhabitants for the first half of the 20th century. On 28 March 1961 No 7007 *Great Western* approaches the station with a Worcester-Paddington express, passing through some delightful but highly rural scenery.

Growth of trees on the short embankment overlooking the station has necessitated a slight move to the left of the original view, but the access ramp links with the view above. Another FGW 'Adelante' heads through the station on 14 July 2005, this time en route to Worcester. Now just a single platform, at least the station is still open for business, though still a long way from habitation and with extremely limited parking space! Note the still very rural setting and that the evidence of the previous up platform and access ramp have been totally swallowed by the passage of time. *John Spencer Gilks/MJS*

HANBOROUGH: The village of Long Handborough was tiny when the railway arrived, but over the passage of the 20th century it grew, with housing and some industrial development, to become a fair-sized community, leading to the retention of its station. Once known as Handborough for Blenheim, the station name was changed in more recent times to Hanborough, without a 'd', despite the village retaining that letter! On 19 October 1957 No 2899 heads a southbound Class H freight through the station towards Oxford. The loop that ran behind the waiting shelter on the left can just be discerned beyond the signal, joining the main line in front of the road overbridge. The up platform, on the right, accommodates a variety of building styles!

Yet another 'Adelante' is captured on the route, this time slowing for the stop at Hanborough, bound for Oxford and, ultimately, Paddington. With the removal of the down platform and all loops and sidings, the area has acquired a much more rural feel, which, with wild flowers and mown lawns on the remaining platform, makes for a pleasing aspect. The summer of 2005 also saw £65,000-worth of improvements, including doubling the car parking spaces to 50, undercover cycle space and new lighting. *R. M. Casserley/MJS*

Kidlington and the Woodstock branch

KIDLINGTON was initially called Woodstock Road when it opened in 1855, but was re-named on 19 May 1890 when the Woodstock branch opened. For long periods the branch trains ran between Woodstock and Kidlington, stabling in the bay platform seen in the lower centre of this view from June 1962. A single box van stands on the siding laid into the Oxfordshire Farmers Bacon Factory in November 1923, then later used by C. & T. Harris (Calne) Ltd until December 1966. The sizeable goods shed to the right of this, originally built to broad gauge (hence the slightly offset track leading into it), was demolished in 1984.

Here is another example of how comprehensively previous infrastructure can be obliterated. Any trace of the station and yard is now buried beneath the subsequent industrial development, with yet another 'out-of-town' trading unit occupying the land on 17 July 2005. Apart from the main line to the left, the only relevant point of reference between these two views is the presence of a gate, on the extreme right, alongside the site entrance road and giving motor access to the lineside. *P. J. Garland, Roger Carpenter collection/MJS*

KIDLINGTON: The branch platform is seen in more detail, again on 27 February 1954, the last day of services to Woodstock. No 1420's smokebox is adorned with two eyes above the number and the message 'Wot No [unidentifiable] Today?' below. The siding to Harris's factory is immediately to the right of No 1420, while, to the left, travellers alight from the single coach, either to join the main-line train or cross the footbridge for a journey to Oxford (this footbridge was removed to near Didcot some time after 1964). Having been a Cardiff (Cathays) loco until transfer just five months prior to this view, No 1420 is here shedded at Oxford, from where it travelled to Southall (1958), Devon, South Wales and, finally, Gloucester, from where it was withdrawn on 22 November 1964.

As a comparative ground-level view was both inaccessible and meaningless, bearing in mind the piles of building materials by the left-hand fence, this is the view from the old A423 Oxford-Banbury road bridge. The previously mentioned vehicle access to the lineside and its gate are seen in clearer definition in the lower right of this view on 17 July 2005. *A. W. V. Mace, Roger Carpenter collection/MJS*

SHIPTON-ON-CHERWELL: A little north of Kidlington the short branch to the tourist Mecca of Woodstock veered westwards from the main line. With Bletchington Cement Works visible in the distance, alongside the main line, No 1442 slows for the stop at Shipton-on-Cherwell Halt, the only station on the branch apart from the terminus. The halt opened as late as 1 April 1929, serving a community barely into three figures and situated around half a mile away, across the busy A423 road and with no direct road access to the station. The branch was closed in its entirety officially on 1 March 1954, with the last train running on 27 February. This view of the single-coach 2.48pm Oxford-Woodstock service was just a fortnight earlier, on 13 February.

This second view of the 2.48pm from Oxford was taken on the last day, 27 February 1954. No 1420 leaves for the short run to Woodstock, unusually sandwiched between two coaches due to the anticipated extra demand. Looking into the sun makes it a less than perfect photograph, but its inherent interest overcomes this. The passengers, complete with pram, having alighted, prepare to make their way home. Note the extremely sparse facilities, with a single platform face and a couple primitive lamps.

Our final look at Shipton is on 11 March 1957, three years after closure. The lamps are without fittings, the station nameboard has gone and grass is springing up. Note the A4095 winding its way in the distance towards Bicester. *P. G. Barlow, Peter Treloar collection/R. J. Buckley, R. M. Casserley collection/ R. M. Casserley*

BLENHEIM & WOODSTOCK's station building sat squat at the side of the main road into the town from Oxford. Though this portrait gives the appearance of health for the station, with cars parked outside in the late-afternoon sunshine and the doors open to the platform, this is in fact the last day of services, 27 February 1954, and it is more likely that visitors are here to be 'in at the death' rather than regularly supporting the branch services. With the huge Blenheim Palace estate almost literally across the road, it is a pity that the branch could not have survived to a time when tourism was to expand dramatically.

Happily, as seen on 17 July 2005, the building has survived almost intact, certainly externally, as Young's Garage & Convenience Store. Two chimneys have gone, as have the iron railings, front awning and central entrance and brickwork, but otherwise little has changed and it has been kept in good repair. The cars on the forecourt make an interesting comparison to those seen above half a century earlier! *A. W. V. Mace, Roger Carpenter collection/MJS*

BLENHEIM & WOODSTOCK station always operated with just the one platform face, but in earlier times there was a track to the short goods platform on the left and, in addition, a run-round facility to release locomotives on incoming trains from the buffer stops. Again seen on the last day of services, No 1420 engages in some shunting, to add a second coach for one of the last ever runs over the branch. Had there been at least this number of travellers on each train in normal service, the branch may have survived longer, especially as freight was quite healthy right up to closure.

Yes, this is the same view! Incredibly, when photographed on 17 July 2005, the station canopy, sheltering the travellers above, is still in situ, now acting as some protection to the line of cars on the right, with added glazing to meet up with the slightly higher roof built over the old trackbed. The far doors mark the old track alignment and, beyond, the end wall of the station still survives. The left-hand wall is roughly in line with the old goods platform. *A. W. V. Mace, Roger Carpenter collection/MJS, courtesy of Young's Garage*

GWR and LNWR lines around Bicester

ARDLEY was located on the other former GWR route running south from Banbury, through Bicester North, and was another station away from the immediate environs of the village it purported to serve. With a thinly populated district surrounding it – only around 200 people lived in the village at the turn of the 20th century – it was graced with two platform loops, two through lines and three sidings, including a cattle pen. One of those sidings, with iron ore hopper wagons awaiting the next delivery from the nearby quarry, can be seen to the left of this view looking south in June 1962. Passenger services ceased on 7 January 1963 and freight ended exactly 18 months later.

The four-track arrangement was dispensed with on 4 November 1968 when the route was singled. Over time, with increasing demand for services following Privatisation, this led to a bottleneck, especially between Banbury and Princes Risborough. After the section from Risborough to Bicester was re-doubled 30 years later, during 1998, 'Project Evergreen' was launched to complete the re-instatement of a twin-track railway to Banbury. Costing some £50 million – actually below the £60 million budgeted! – this work was completed during 2002. A comparison view is seen here on 3 March 2002, with the A43 road bridge the common feature. Preparatory work is under way, with a delivery of steel sleepers piled at the side of the single line. It hardly seems possible that there used to be four tracks here! *Lens of Sutton collection/MJS*

Seen at around the time of withdrawal of passenger services, the substantial 63-lever signal box was located on the northern end of the down platform. It closed with the singling of the route in November 1968. *Lens of Sutton collection*

BICESTER NORTH is seen on a misty 27 February 1957, looking towards Princes Risborough. The station, opened on 1 July 1910, was used to the sight of a slip coach being left from a speeding northbound express at certain times of the day; on the right is the water column that would replenish the locomotive that would then retrieve the coach and bring it into the station. Note the substantial goods shed in the distance.

Nearly half a century later the basic layout of the station is unchanged – it had not been affected by the 1968 rationalisation, apart from removal of the through lines. However, the footbridge has had its roof removed, but lifts have been added. The water column and goods shed have gone, but the station now boasts cycle racks, 'rear view' mirrors to assist train drivers, and a recent revamp and repaint. The station nameboard now proudly announces 'Welcome to Bicester North. Alight here for Bicester Village', the latter being a huge shopping village that has recently become popular with visitors from China! *R. M. Casserley/MJS*

BICESTER NORTH: An example of the slip coach mentioned opposite is seen here on 31 May 1960 after being released from the 5.10pm Paddington-Wolverhampton (Low Level) train, which roared through the station non-stop. No 4907 *Broughton Hall* has coupled up and is moving forward to the points before backing into the platform, both to release passengers wanting Bicester and also to attach it to its own northbound train, the 4.34pm semi-fast Paddington-Wolverhampton. The service, which was the last such facility in the country, finally succumbed to the economists and changing ideas within British Railways less than four months later, on 9 September.

The comparative view on 17 July 2005 is nowhere near as inherently arresting as the above view, especially with the absence of steam and semaphore signals, but the view is not devoid of interest. The substantial colour light signal in the centre of the view, installed during 'Project Evergreen', is bi-directional and also controls access to the newly installed holding siding, to the right of the running lines in this view, in the middle distance. Its number, 'ME2033', signifies control from Marylebone and shows how many such signals are thus controlled from the Metropolis! *Michael Mensing/MJS*

BICESTER NORTH: Looking in the opposite direction, we can see the goods shed at the end of the down platform, removed following the closure of the goods yard on 7 September 1964. In this view from 17 February 1963, an unidentified Class 52 'Western' diesel-hydraulic express locomotive approaches the station with another Paddington-Wolverhampton service, but this time without a slip coach! In the centre, No 6169 stands 'wrong line' on the up through track with a very short ballast train. The substantial 67-lever signal box closed on 27 October 1968.

The view on 17 July 2005 shows great change. The through tracks are absent, as is the signal box and much of the previous infrastructure. Evidence of infilling of the previous rodding space under the platform by the signal box is seen in the lighter-coloured brickwork on the up platform. At the end of this and the nearside down platform, extensions have been added to cope with the possibility of longer trains following growth in passenger numbers locally. At this date, through services to Marylebone were obstructed by the now infamous tunnel collapse under a proposed Tesco supermarket at Gerrards Cross, so No 165012, here on its way north, is only shuttling between Beaconsfield and Birmingham. The tunnel re-opened on 20 August. *John Spencer Gilks/MJS*

BICESTER LONDON ROAD opened in 1850 on the LNWR's cross-country Oxford-Bletchley route, and was of sturdy stone construction. In this scene from 1905, an LNWR steam railcar pauses at the station for the benefit of photographer and any potential customers. The station had low platforms and this railcar, standing in the Oxford-bound platform, had a mechanism that swung out three steps and a handrail for use by passengers at 'rail-level' halts.

The wider view from 3 June 1956 shows more of the main station building and the timber-clad waiting shelter on the opposite platform. The crossing signal box can be seen at the far end of the latter, looking towards Bletchley. An unusual visitor on this day is No WD113, a saddle-tank from the local MoD site, giving a trip to members of the Birmingham Locomotive Club.

Between the late 1950s and this view of 17 July 2005, fate dealt a varied hand to the station. Closed to passenger traffic by BR on 1 January 1968, it re-opened under the auspices of Network SouthEast in May 1987. The attractive station buildings survived, but were in private hands and, as a consequence, facilities for the travelling public were basic, to put it mildly! By the time of re-opening, the line had been singled and the Oxford platform removed, with the old trackbed left as a long headshunt. A waiting shelter was provided alongside the old buildings in the early 1990s, but the shameful permission to demolish the latter saw them progressively dismantled, to leave only part of the platform-facing wall by 1995. Ten years on and they stand as an ugly reminder of a once delightful structure. Somewhat thankfully, however, the track has been renewed, there are seats once more and the railway property has seen the **paintbrush!** *Roger Carpenter collection/John Edgington/MJS*

BICESTER LONDON ROAD: Looking in the opposite direction, this was the view towards Oxford around 1962, with the stone station buildings and goods shed beyond still standing. Note the two sidings beyond the wooden goods shed, the open nature of the approach road complete with arc-roofed shed, and the 'London Road' addendum to the station nameboard tacked on to the frame.

In the 'present' view, also from 17 July 2005, the wanton destruction of past heritage is palpably obvious, with the ugly remains of the station building standing like some grotesque Hollywood film set and all evidence of the Oxford platform and waiting shelter, to the left, and the sidings, to the right, obliterated. There have been constant rumours of re-opening the line throughout to Bletchley, Bedford and on to Cambridge, and if these come to fruition it is to be hoped that a new station building can be provided here. *Lens of Sutton collection/MJS*

LAUNTON was the most easterly station on this route within the county boundary. Not only was the area extremely rural and sparsely populated – and still largely is today, despite the increase in population in general, the massive growth in Bicester town and the presence of the MoD site – but the station was again like so many throughout the UK, situated some distance from the locality after which it was named, in this case more than a mile! In another picture from around 1962, looking towards Bletchley, the country road out of Launton to Poundon and Stratton Andley crosses the line. A short spur siding ran behind the right-hand dwellings until 30 November 1959. A Ladies Waiting Room is provided, together with steps to assist passengers on to and from the low platform. The house at the end of the nearside platform acted as both Booking Office and staff accommodation, including crossing keeper duties. It became a private residence in 1976 when automatic crossing lights were fitted.

The comparative view on 17 July 2005 shows the lights protecting the roadway, and the single line. To the casual eye there has never been a station here, but the presence of the low platform, with its edge still visible beneath the encroaching undergrowth, gives the game away, approaching 40 years since closure to passenger traffic. *Lens of Sutton collection/MJS*

The rudimentary Ladies Waiting Room and the wooden steps – to assist with the low platforms, wooden on this side – are again seen in this view on Sunday 9 August 1959. No 80043 slows for the station stop with the Sundays-only 4.43pm Oxford-Bletchley local service. Allocated new to Bletchley exactly seven years earlier, the loco was removed from the area shortly after this view, moving to the SR in the week ending 5 December. Thereafter staying on ex-Southern metals, it was withdrawn on 27 March 1966, less than 14 years old – no age for a steam locomotive! Some spot re-sleepering appears to have been recently completed, with wooden sleepers in front of the train compared with the concrete versions on this side. *Mike Mitchell, MJS collection*

ISLIP: Apart from six halts, Islip was the only station between Bicester London Road and the ex-LNWR station at Oxford Rewley Road. Opened on 1 October 1850, it was this time situated closer to its eponymous habitation than many of its contemporaries, and consequently attracted healthy levels of traffic, not least with locally produced milk, even on a Sunday! In this undated view, probably from the late 1950s, three new noticeboards stand on the Oxford-bound platform, perhaps to replace those on the fencing further along the platform. The view is after 1956, as evidenced by the box containing signalling instruments being on the side wall, partly hidden in this view by the seven-lever ground frame. Access to the station was by an inclined approach from the B4027 road crossing

the bridge seen right of centre, with travellers reaching this nearside platform via the barrow crossing, a situation common to most of the route. There were once sidings here on the left, the turnout for which can just be seen in the bottom left-hand corner.

As with Bicester, when the route was closed to passengers in 1968 Islip was without a rail service until the initially experimental re-introduction in 1987. This is the view of the facilities provided by Network SouthEast and still in use on 17 July 2005, with just a short platform, recognising the local nature of the traffic. The sidings have long gone, as has the Bletchley-bound platform, with alternative use and nature removing any traces. The B-road bridge is just visible beyond the far end of the platform. *MJS collection/MJS*

ISLIP: Looking in the other direction from the Bletchley-bound platform, this view from 30 December 1967, just two days before closure, shows the site of the sidings and goods shed, beyond the far end of the opposite platform, now just an open space. The goods shed was in use until 7 September 1964. The station is now looking distinctly tatty, with wooden fencing needing attention and the posters largely devoid of information.

The comparative view from 17 July 2005 shows just how much has been swept away – the single track, modern-style waiting shelter and complete lack of any freight facilities in the 21st century tell their own story. At least the bright paintwork and surrounding greenery lend a pleasing ambience while one waits for a train! *Edwin Wilmshurst/MJS*

Oxford Rewley Road

OXFORD REWLEY ROAD: While the GWR was first into Oxford, initially with a terminal station south of the city, then a later, more central facility, the LNWR was not far behind, with ambitions for a foothold in the city. Arriving on 20 May 1851, the new station was literally next door to what would become the GWR's through station 17 months later, but was somewhat strangely named 'Rewley Road', after the small side street next to it, rather than, say, 'Park End', after the main A420 road into the city centre! Parts of the station were designed and even erected by Joseph Paxton, designer of the Crystal Palace, and some of this is reflected in the modular cast-iron construction, albeit that the frontage originally had a roof span extending outwards and with four pillars rather than the two seen here. Passenger services ended on 1 October 1951, just over a century from opening, and the station building was then home to a hostel for railwaymen and later, up to closure, a tyre centre. Rewley Road was between the station front and the pitched-roof building beyond.

This is perhaps the shot that shows the greatest change in the whole of this collection! Following the removal of the old station, the whole road layout on this extremely busy thoroughfare into the city centre was remodelled from 1999. The streaming of road traffic was altered from the previous layout and an outpost of Oxford University – the Said Business School – was built on much of the site, not without controversy and its critics! This was the view on 13 June 2005, as close as possible to the original spot – and only possible with knowledge of where the station had been sited, for even many of the surrounding buildings have been swept away! Traffic lights shine brightly under the glowering skies. *Roger Carpenter, Lens of Sutton collection/MJS*

OXFORD REWLEY ROAD: Seen in its death throes, the Grade II-listed station was, thankfully, not merely demolished, which would indeed have been a crime, but taken down 'brick by brick' and transported to the Quainton Road site of the Buckinghamshire Railway Centre. Seen here on 14 December 1998, viewed from the opposite side to the previous page, scaffolding holds the edifice in place while the removal gathers pace. It was re-erected at Quainton Road the following year and now forms a very valuable part of the visitor experience at the new site.

Once more the transformation is dramatic and complete. On 13 June 2005 the Said Business School stands boldly on the site, with a mini-race-track outside on the realigned roadway, with the A420 road underbridge centre left and the remaining Oxford station to its right. Hundreds of commuters' bicycles stand by the trees outside the station, awaiting their owners' return. *Both MJS*

OXFORD REWLEY ROAD: This view inside the station in the late 19th century shows an oval booking office at the end of the platform and the low pre-1906 platforms. Note the large domed gas lamps.

With the construction of the Said Business School, the opportunity to attempt a present-day view was lost and would have been meaningless, so we have a second, later view inside the station trainshed. Standing beneath the 'Crystal Palace' roof, the LMS experimental diesel unit is the object of much interest on 17 September 1938 – five days after the start of a trial. Looking decidedly futuristic for the time, it plied its trade for a period between Oxford, Bletchley and Cambridge, in an attempt to assess the practicalities of such units working and reducing operating costs on branch lines. *MJS collection/F. C. LeManquais, MJS collection*

OXFORD REWLEY ROAD: After the cessation of passenger traffic, regular freight traffic continued until well into the 1970s. This is a view from around 1962, looking from the goods yard towards the former passenger station, with one platform face occupied by box vans, sidings to the left and the ex-LNWR goods shed to the right. The yard was in use until as late as 5 April 1984.

It is now virtually impossible to stand in the shoes of the 'past' photographer, but this is as close as your author was able to be, with the rear of the Said Business School dominating the scene and hiding every vestige of the past under its bulk. Pleasant gardens they may be, but with nowhere near the charisma to a railway enthusiast of the previous incarnation! *Lens of Sutton collection/MJS*

OXFORD (LNWR) SHED: The exit from Rewley Road station was by way of a narrow throat on a swing bridge across a connection between the River Thames and the Oxford Canal, almost opposite the site of the GWR engine shed. Just past this restricted passage, the Buckinghamshire Railway sited its own engine shed from 1851, after an earlier one closer to the station had been removed with site improvements. This was blown down in 1877, rebuilt, then closed in 1882, to be replaced by a two-road facility with a northlight slate roof. This lasted until closure on 3 December 1950, with demolition around 1962. In this view from across the canal on 3 October 1948, three ex-LNWR '7F' 0-8-0s rest between duties.

Moving across into the shed yard, the brick-based, dead-end, northlight shed is seen in closer detail on 24 October 1937. LMS No 9596, one of Fowler's 1929 class of '7F' 0-8-0s, developed from the LNWR type seen above, stands by the large water tank before returning eastwards to the LMS system. Despite externally looking in fine condition here, No 9596 was not one of the class to survive into Nationalisation in 1948.

Our third view of the shed area shows the more general layout, with 'Watford Tank' No 6936 occupying one of the two main routes into the station, and the tower of St Barnabas Church in the distance, on the other side of the canal. This ex-LNWR class of '2P' 0-6-2Ts became extinct on 21 March 1953, but sadly No 6936 was another casualty before Nationalisation in 1948. The GWR main line northwards out of Oxford can be seen on the extreme left. *P. M. Alexander, Millbrook House collection/Norman Glover, Alan Wycherley collection/E. Johnson, Roger Carpenter collection*

OXFORD REWLEY ROAD GOODS YARD: Not the normal fare in Oxford, but on 29 April 1960 the ex-LMS goods yard, between the LMS and GWR station sites, is the temporary home to ex-Caledonian Railway No 123 and ex-GWR *City of Truro*. The well-kept Rewley Road station, here in industrial use, can be seen to the left, while the large building in the background was occupied by Frank Cooper, the famous producer of marmalade based in Oxford. Of the small number of visitors seen here, a high proportion are railwaymen, obviously intrigued in comparing the styles of two distinct railways.

The Frank Cooper building and its immediate neighbour are still present in this view from 17 July 2005, but once more the slab-sided Said Business School completely dominates the skyline. Note how the space between the two erstwhile station sites has been commandeered for access to the remaining ex-GWR facility, but this does not show the number of changes of ideas for this area that have existed over the years! *Peter Treloar/MJS*

Oxford General

OXFORD GENERAL: We start our look at the city's principal station just to the south, where a footbridge crosses the ex-GWR main line; allowing locals to avoid a long detour to reach the city centre, the bridge links Osney Lane and Becket Street, and in former times passed by the cemetery on one side and the cattle pens and sidings adjacent to Becket Street on the other. The former is seen here to the right of No 73111 as it approaches the Oxford stop with a Bournemouth-York cross-country service on 31 March 1964. Officially allocated to 70A (Nine Elms) shed in London at the time, and thus a strange visitor on this train, the absence of a shedplate on the loco's smokebox could indicate an impending move. Its next official transfer was to Basingstoke depot on 14 September 1964, from where it was withdrawn on 31 October 1965, just ten years old! After arrival in Oxford, No 73111 will be removed for turning and servicing on the nearby shed before returning south with a similar service. An ex-GWR engine will most likely have taken the train forward.

On a dull evening of 13 June 2005, an exact comparison is frustrated by the tree growth hiding the cemetery. A few steps to the left, therefore, shows the 21st-century version of the cross-country service, with tilting No 221136 *Yuri Gagarin* arriving with Virgin Trains 1E45 1746 Bournemouth-Leeds service. Note how private enterprise and some reclamation by nature have forcefully encroached on to the edge of the remaining railway, following the closure of the once-important South Goods Yard and the demolition of the goods shed in 1985. *Paul Chancellor collection/MJS*

OXFORD GENERAL: From this angle, slightly further along the footbridge, the extent of the cemetery can be more easily judged, as No 6125 brings a local passenger duty towards Oxford station around 1958. A rake of empty coal wagons occupies the siding on the left. Based in and around London in the first years after Nationalisation, No 6125 then moved to South Wales for a little short of two years, from July 1960 to April 1962, before returning to the Metropolis and finally Slough shed, from where it was withdrawn on 23 January 1965.

A comparative view nearly two decades later sees No 47252 operating a Southern to Midland inter-region service on 4 October 1975. Note that, in the ten years since the upper view opposite, the Goods Shed has lost its rails to the short dock platform, which itself has been removed and replaced with a Portakabin. A gate now bars entrance to the shed itself and fencing segregates the site from the remaining tracks. Two engineer's trains, with ballast and track panels, wait in the sidings, obviously to undertake some weekend possession work in the vicinity. No 47252 was renumbered 47615 on 18 June 1984, named *Castell Caerffili/ Caerphilly Castle* on 30 April 1985, renumbered again on 25 April 1994, to 47747, with three further names – *Res Publica* (until 2000), *Graham Farish* (until 2002) and *Florence Nightingale* thereafter! It lay in store in 2005.

The present scene is relatively devoid of much interest, either on or near the tracks. By 17 July 2005 requirements on the Paddington-Oxford route were largely met by the later versions of the Thames 'Turbos', and one such, No 166210, slows for the station stop forming the 2N24 First Great Western Link 0948 service from Paddington. With natural and man-made encroachments on both sides of the tracks, the railway now has a far more hemmed-in feel. *Peter Treloar/Tom Heavyside/MJS*

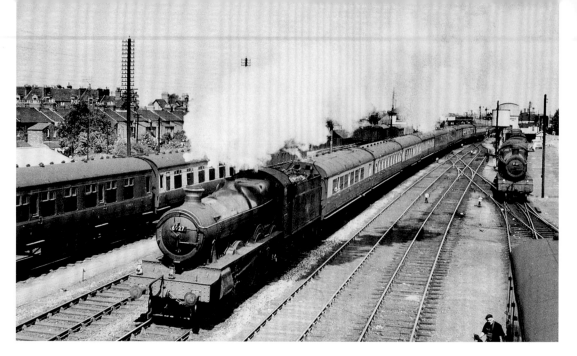

OXFORD GENERAL: Now looking north from the same footbridge, the view towards the station shows much more interest, with sidings each side of the main line and attendant engine/stock movements. In this undated view, but thought to be the summer of 1958, No 6927 *Lilford Hall* makes a leisurely restart from Oxford with its nine-coach load, its headcode indicating empty coaching stock. Wearing an 81D (Reading) shedplate, this was possibly shortly before its transfer to Oxford on 12 July. If the timing is correct, No 4907 *Broughton Hall*, backing on to a rake of box vans on the right, is ex-Oxford, having moved to Slough the previous March.

With slightly more explosive exhaust, No 92103 treads the same road on 31 March 1964, this time with a decidedly mixed Class H freight, conveying all manner of goods southwards. With the view on the left no longer hidden by coaching stock, the surrounding sidings and infrastructure can be seen. New in September 1956 and allocated to Toton shed, between Nottingham and Derby, No 92103 was at this time a 15C (Leicester Midland) engine. A subsequent move to Birkenhead came on 10 April 1965, from where it was withdrawn on 15 July 1967, a year from the end of steam on BR. *Peter Treloar/Paul Chancellor collection*

OXFORD GENERAL: This typical view of a train leaving Oxford in steam days was taken from the Osney Lane steps up to the footbridge. No 7027 *Thornbury Castle* really puts in the effort as it restarts an evening Worcester-Paddington express on 23 May 1963. More of the traditional railway infrastructure is seen here, including the 57-lever Oxford Station South signal box and, above the train, two water towers, the largest for locomotives standing in the station and the smaller one, which was once topped by a typical GWR cowl, for those using the Becket Street yard. The signal box was replaced in 1973, with others in the area, by a power box that stands on the previous site of the bay to the down platform.

The passage of more than 40 years and changing fortunes and fashions for the local railway has not been overly kind to Oxford, with much of the railway land south of the station put to other uses. The signal box has gone; just two of the sidings remain, although not used for some time; semaphores and water towers have long since disappeared; and, on the right, the previous goods yard, which initially became a car scrapyard when taken out of railway use, is now a well-maintained but expensive car park. Two examples of First Great Western's front-line motive power are present on 13 June 2005 – an HST (left) works northwards, while the latest addition to the route, 'Adelante' No 180106, leaves the platform and prepares to regain the main line with the 1F74 FGWL 1816 Worcester (Shrub Hill)-Paddington service. Note the appearance of a glazed footbridge, opened on 8 April 1990 to replace the sometimes overcrowded and less-than-ideal subway previously used.
Geoff King/MJS

OXFORD GENERAL: The approach to Oxford's GWR station has seen many and varied alterations over the years, both to accommodate rebuilding of the station itself and also the incessant increase in bus, taxi and private vehicle traffic. On a higher level than the A420 from which it is accessed, there has always been a rising gradient to the station, presenting particular problems for the planners. Seen here around 1967, this wooden edifice had served the city since 1891, and at the time of this shot was beginning to really show signs of its age. It was demolished in 1971, to be replaced with a structure that proved more temporary, being itself replaced by a brand new, attractively styled facility in 1990. Note the proliferation of signs and the delightful array of cars.

While the station itself has remained largely untouched – certainly externally – since opening in 1990, the approach to it has undergone more rethinking, not least regarding the potential conflict between traffic leaving the station and that passing the exit and heading into the city centre. The building of the Said Business School has added its own influence and the final layout (as at 17 July 2005) is seen here, with a bus interchange next to the station entrance and the previous height differential smoothed by making people climb steps to the station from a slightly lowered road level. *Roger Carpenter/MJS*

OXFORD GENERAL: This wonderful view of the old station, then known as Oxford General, was taken just over halfway through its active life. Looking south on 17 October 1935, the picture is so full of interest that the viewer hardly knows where to start! As well as the scissors crossovers between platform and through lines – a modeller's delight (or nightmare?) – the differing levels of canopy on the far side, from the 1910 extension of the up platform, are obvious, as is the slightly more subtle change to the platform facing. Signs abound – 'Take Bovril or Take the Consequences' (!), 'Cuticura Soap', 'Mitchells & Butlers', and one extolling the delights of Brighton as a destination – together with those directing passengers to the various departments. Parcels are well in evidence, including a wicker basket designated 'GWR Hotels Dept Dept Paddington', and there is a bookstall and a 'Luncheon and Dining Room'. The inter-war travellers were certainly well looked after. The previously seen large water tank stands at the southern end of the platform. *MJS collection*

OXFORD GENERAL: That substantial water tank at the southern end of the station is seen in greater detail here, on 10 July 1965, as No 6870 *Bodicote Grange* pauses with yet another cross-country service, the 9.40am Birmingham (Snow Hill)-Portsmouth eight-coach train. A Brush Type 4 diesel approaches on the through track, but it will be held at the signals, as the 'Grange' has 'right away' from the starter signal. Comparison with a post-First World War view would show a different tank on the brick superstructure and the signal gantry affixed to the track side of the tower, rather than free-standing by the road bridge as here.

With the menacing clouds restricting the summer evening light, 'Adelante' No 180104 presents the modern face of London-bound services, here operating as the 2P92 FGWL 2045 Oxford-Paddington semi-fast service. To the left, 'Turbo' No 166207 arrives as the 1D69 FGWL 1950 Paddington-Banbury service. The main signal gantry superstructure remains intact, but now carries colour light signals. The controlled access across the tracks remains, but we now have steel girder strengthening for the bridge over the A420, following the raising of the bridge in 1979. There is also a sign wisely cautioning 'Limited Clearance'. *Edwin Wilmshurst/MJS, with permission*

OXFORD GENERAL: Back on the down platform, we turn to look at trains arriving from the south. On 24 September 1955 No 2841 climbs the gradient into the through road with a down fitted freight, passing Station South signal box on the right, with the headcode denoting the possible presence of perishables. An Oxley engine at this time, No 2841 spent most of its post-1948 life in the West Midlands/Worcester area until a move to Reading on 3 October 1959. A move to Southall came on 6 April 1963, from where it was withdrawn eight months later.

Just short of ten years later, superficially little has changed, with only the height of the far bridge parapet reduced and the addition of another 'Limited Clearance' notice on the extreme right being the obvious differences. Spotters on the end of the platform record the passage of No 44841 on the through road on a Portsmouth-Wolverhampton cross-country working on 17 July 1965. Following a stay at Nottingham shed until 3 November 1951, the ex-LMS 'Black 5' was another resident of the West Midlands and of Oxley shed at the date of this view. The end came from that shed on 5 November 1966.

By 13 June 2005 the passing of 40 years has seen both much and little change! To the left, the water tower is no more, the bridge parapet has again been altered, with the addition of an adjacent pedestrian walkway to the car park, the steel reinforcement has appeared on the road bridge, and there are detail differences at track level, but elsewhere much is at it was before. No 220030 *Devon Voyager* arrives at the station with the 1M31 Virgin Trains 2005 Reading-Manchester Piccadilly service. *Geoff King/Frank Cassell/ MJS*

OXFORD GENERAL: A look across from the down platform on 24 September 1955 shows just one of the delights that could await the spotter or enthusiast at this time. One of the fast-dwindling SR's celebrated 'Remembrance' Class still finds important duty at the head of a York-Bournemouth cross-country service, departing from Oxford with its Eastern Region coaching stock, having taken over from what was probably an ER engine that has brought in the train. Withdrawal of No 32327 *Trevithick* came within four months, from Basingstoke shed. The original water tank is in situ, with the gantry bolted to the main structure, the Becket Street goods yard is healthily occupied, and the city's gasholder is three-quarters full.

As we have already seen, the view today looks bare by comparison to happier times, with the water tower absent, colour lights instead of semaphores and the absence of goods yard and even gas holder! Three-car 'Turbo' No 166211 begins a journey to Paddington as the delayed 2000 departure, while in the distance No 220030 *Devon Voyager* (seen on page 63) approaches. *Geoff King/MJS*

Opposite page OXFORD GENERAL: Standing at roughly the same point as the previous page, but looking in the opposite direction, the increasingly stained and weary-looking, long-suffering station is visited by No 5049 *Earl of Plymouth* on 10 October 1962. It is about to work the 5.30pm 'rush hour' service to Paddington. Note the luxury of eight carriages, the number of cycles left on the platform, and the signal gantry attached to the down platform canopy. A well-travelled locomotive over recent years, back and forth between Devon and South Wales, No 5049 was here allocated to St Philips Marsh shed in Bristol, from where it was withdrawn less than six months after this view, on 6 April 1963.

A little over 2½ years later, diesels have taken over the cross-country duties through Oxford. On 17 July 1965 D5858 arrives with the 8.42am Bradford-Poole service – with an apparently incorrect reporting number! – slowing for the stop alongside the even blacker and unattractive canopy. New just four days before the view of No 5049 above, and allocated to 41A (Sheffield Darnall) shed, D5858 was still resident of that depot when working this train. An ER loco for much of its life, it was renumbered 31323 in November 1973, withdrawn from Stratford on 5 March 1988, re-instated nine days later, and finally despatched on 8 June 1989.

A slightly wider view gives an opportunity to see the improvements brought by the new 1990 station, with its smart lines and the substantial covered footbridge. In the up platform, No 166211 is again seen as the delayed 1F76 FGWL 2000 departure for Paddington, while on the left sister unit No 166203 has arrived from the capital and is now empty stock, ready to move into the holding sidings just north of the station. Note the re-instatement of a crossover between the through lines compared with the two earlier views. *David Holmes/Frank Cassell/MJS*

On 18 October 1986 what was to become something of a temporary rebuild to the station is glimpsed to the right of No 47372 heading for Didcot on a 'merry-go-round' train. The subway is still in use and it has to be said that the 'new' station was not a thing of great beauty! Unremarkable as it may seem to an untutored eye, the use of a Class 47 on these coal trains was highly unusual and one can only surmise that No 47372 was deputising for a failed Class 58 loco. New from Brush Works, as D1891, on 6 August 1965, a few weeks before the centre picture opposite was taken, it became No 47372 under the TOPS renumbering in February 1974. Again on the ER/NER for much of its life, it outlived many of its contemporaries by becoming No 57314 on 25 October 2004, as one of Virgin Trains' 'Thunderbird' locomotives, to assist failed electric traction, etc. It also acquired the name *Fire Fly. MJS*

Gt Western Ry   Gt Western Ry
Barnstaple G.W   Barnstaple G.W
TO
OXFORD
via Dulverton Somerton Westbury Yeovil & Didcot
THIRD CLASS
26/9 C   Fare   26/9 C
OXFORD   OXFORD
FOR CONDITIONS SEE BACK (W.L

This page and opposite above OXFORD GENERAL: Now at the north end of the down platform, we witness a smartly turned out No 7023 *Penrice Castle* at precisely 4.46pm, drifting to a stand with the 3.15pm Paddington-Hereford service on 10 October 1962. Although built to the GWR design, No 7023 was in truth a British Railways engine, new as late as 31 July 1949. Initially allocated to Cardiff Canton, it stayed there until 13 August 1960, when it moved to Worcester, the depot that was home to it when seen here. Withdrawal came in February 1965, from Oxley shed. Note the hustle and bustle and paraphernalia on both platforms, but especially on the far side, where a diesel shunter busies itself with parcels vans.

An almost identical view from 17 July 1965 sees another diesel shunter similarly occupied, the station looking almost unchanged, and the same service as above – the 1T13 3.15pm out of Paddington – but the motive power is vastly different and the train will now just go to Worcester. Drawing to a halt as the spotters record the number in their notebooks, D1748 is just three days short of one year old. Its early days were spent working from 81A (Old Oak Common) shed, but here it is now a Bristol Bath Road loco. Going on to become No 47155 in February 1974, it later became 47660 on 18 December 1986, 47815 on 31 August 1989 and was named *Abertawe/Landore* in Swansea on 1 July 2000. This name was removed in December 2004, when the relatively new Cotswold Rail inherited the loco.

Just short of 40 years later, on 13 June 2005, the left-hand side of the station has seen little disturbance from the 1990 rebuilding, with the 1910 extension still largely intact, with minor refurbishment and reshaping of the roof timbers since 1965. There is now a canopy over the far platforms, but appearances are deceptive with the parcels vans standing there, as they are now permanent fixtures, with all parcels traffic taken away from rail. The view this side shows just how much has been swept away with the more recent designs, leaving waiting passengers far more exposed to the elements. The new order is again seen here, with 'Adelante' 'class leader' No 180101 restarting the 1D65 FGWL 1918 Paddington-Great Malvern service from the Oxford stop. *David Holmes/Frank Cassell/MJS*

Below A brief moment to simply wallow in nostalgia! On an unidentified winter's day in 1958, No 5088 *Llanthony Abbey* waits for the road at the north end of Oxford's down platform, while the driver and fireman have a brief chat. The firebox has a healthy glow and presumably the hosepipe dangling over the cabside, with a trickle of water emanating from it, has just been used to dampen down any coal dust. A Wolverhampton Stafford Road loco for the whole of its British Railways life, it was finally withdrawn on 8 September 1962. It certainly looks a well-kept engine in this view. *MJS collection*

OXFORD GENERAL: The tower of St Barnabas is again prominent as a landmark in this view of No 5932 *Haydon Hall*, 'relegated' to hauling a very mixed up Class H through freight, containing wooden and steel wagons, coal empties, an oil container and box vans, crossing the stream linking river and canal. On an undated view from 1958, multifarious semaphores control the northward exit from the station, complete with secondary route indicators and slotted signals. To the left, the large wooden engine shed building can just be seen.

Another up mixed freight, still with the odd wooden wagon, has more appropriate motive power. No 3849 is crossing that same stream on 6 April 1963, past Oxford Station North signal box, hidden from view above by the loco's exhaust. Note that, with the passage of time, the signals have now been grouped on to a gantry, the number of route indicators has grown and St Barnabas's tower has had its top redesigned.

The most obvious change over the ensuing 40 or so years is the removal of the semaphore gantry and its replacement with far fewer colour lights, the disappearance of the signal box following replacement by the new power box in 1973, and the redevelopment of the ex-LNWR land beyond. This has more recently been extensively developed, with the housing seen here. The steel supports over the stream have also seen change. On 13 June 2005 'Turbo' No 166211 runs into the up platform to form the 2000 service to Paddington. *Peter Treloar/Edwin Wilmshurst/MJS*

OXFORD GENERAL: This is the same view north from Oxford but from the up platform. In the last months of 1958 No 6915 *Mursley Hall* enters the station with an unidentified Class A express, probably bound for Paddington, while on the right some stock movement is being undertaken. Note again the signals and the roof of the engine shed to the left. Here allocated to 81E (Didcot) shed – from 4 October 1958 – subsequent movements were to Shrewsbury (25 February 1961) and Banbury (18 July 1964), from where it was withdrawn on 28 March 1965.

Seventeen years later there has been much change. Not only has steam completely disappeared from the daily scene, but so have the signal gantry and the engine shed (demolished in 1968). The site of the latter is now more of a stabling point than a proper shed, as seen in this view on 4 October 1975. Station North signal box (called Engine Shed signal box until 1942) was nominally replaced in 1973 by the new power box, but does appear here to be still occupied! No 31260 enters with another unidentified inter-regional service, this time bound for a destination on the Western Region.

A very bare sight compared to either of the two above, this is what the modern railway offers. As a Freightliner train roars north behind No 66537 in the fading light of 13 June 2005, the gap in the consist allows us to see that the shed area has been totally swept clean of recognisable infrastructure, replaced by 'Turbo Ted's Nursery' (!) and recent housing development. Just beyond the locomotive are the remains of part of the yard, used for stabling stock, mirrored on the right, where a 'Turbo' unit can be seen. *Peter Treloar/Tom Heavyside/MJS*

OXFORD GENERAL: Before leaving the station complex, we take a final look at the bay platforms at the north end in 1960. In the distance, on the far side of the through lines, two DMU sets stand on what had been the Woodstock branch platform line and the adjacent holding siding, while in the foreground a slightly unusual visitor is seen on the east side of the station, having arrived with a local service from Bletchley. New in 1951, No 42106 was initially allocated to sheds on the Southern Region, finally moving regions to Bletchley shed on 5 December 1959, and to Willesden on 12 December 1964, from where it was dispensed with on 19 June 1965. *MJS collection*

Opposite page OXFORD (GWR) SHED: One slightly unusual feature of the engine shed at Oxford was the positioning of a water tank high up in the roof of the 1875 lifting shop. Constructed of corrugated iron, the shop and the positioning of the water tank both seem rather precarious in this summer view from the early 1960s. The temporary abandonment of braziers, the ancient-looking wooden lamppost and the less than ideal conditions underfoot all lend to the general air of impending closure, which finally came on 3 January 1966. The tender of an LMR 'Black 5', waiting to return home, stands alongside.

After closure to steam, the shed was given over to diesels, both locomotives, including main-line and shunting types, and units. The steam shed buildings were demolished and the new layout was a much simpler affair but, incredibly, the old water tank survived when the lifting shop was pulled down! It is seen here on the left, beyond the two fuel tanks. A small servicing shed stands in the centre, while on the right, on 23 April 1987, No 47033 is a visitor. This basic layout lasted for many years, even after most refuelling was transferred to Reading in 1984, but sadly by the 21st century much had changed, with new housing to the left of this view and the water tank gone. *Norman Kneale/MJS*

OXFORD (GWR) SHED: The view west to east across the shed yard, towards the main line, witnesses the crew of No 34047 *Callington* using their muscle on the turntable, turning their charge in preparation for returning south with a cross-country (probably York-Bournemouth) service. The lifting shop is seen to the right, while on the left No 92216 is a visitor from Southall shed. Seen in the early summer of 1965, No 34047 had been a well-travelled locomotive in its relatively short life, but had been resident at Bournemouth depot since 14 June 1959, although being devoid of a shedplate here. It was withdrawn from there on 9 July 1967 at the very end of steam on the SR.

On the same day three unidentified locomotives occupy the eastern road of the double-sided coaling stage. Provided in 1944, together with many additional sidings to cope with war demands and, specifically, the forthcoming D-Day, it served the shed well after the end of hostilities. Despite being devoid of identifying number, the pannier tank is coaled and in steam – although with some leaks by the look of it! Note the water tank and the modern-looking Oxford North Junction signal box on the far side of the main line. *Both Norman Kneale*

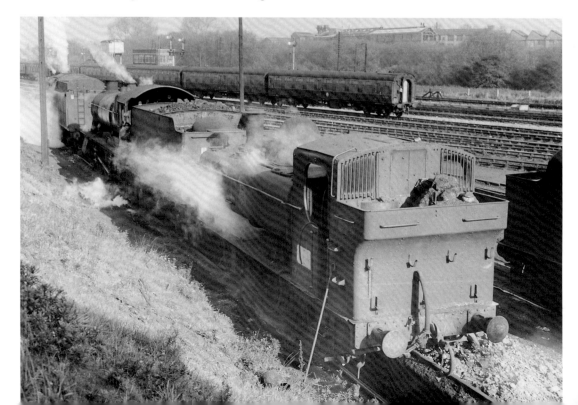

Above OXFORD (GWR) SHED: Again on the same day in 1965 a Standard Class 4 waits to leave the shed yard while a double-headed empty oil train, with D6527 – new in November 1960 and here allocated to 71A (Eastleigh) shed – leading, approaches the station. With these diesels being SR-allocated, this is likely to be a train bound for the Fawley oil terminal. Note the wide expanse of land occupied by both the shed and the carriage sidings. *Norman Kneale*

Below Finally, we are at the north end of the shed yard, looking back. No 4105 accelerates away from the station, gathering speed as it passes the shed and adding to the general smoke haze with a three-coach local service for Banbury on 23 May 1963. Another loco without a shedplate on the smokebox door, it was a Banbury resident at this time, although previously a servant of numerous sheds following Nationalisation, including Oxford in 1953. It was withdrawn from Banbury on 22 February 1964. *Geoff King*

North from Oxford to Yarnton

OXFORD NORTH JUNCTION: By moving slightly further north from the top of Oxford shed yard, we can obtain a greater impression of the extent of the yard and the railway land in this area. Looking south from Walton Well Road on 24 September 1955, No 5935 *Norton Hall* is seen gently accelerating away from the station with a Weymouth-Wolverhampton inter-regional service. The double-sided coaling stage can be seen in the middle of the yard, in the right distance. A Didcot engine at the time, No 5935 later moved to St Philips Marsh (June 1958), Westbury (May 1959) and Radyr (December 1961), from where it was withdrawn on 19 May 1962. Note the spotter on his cycle next to a side stream from the Thames that passes directly under where the 'Hall' has been captured.

Even a cursory look easily identifies this as the same view, with the stream bridge's railings, the main line and even some of the shed's carriage sidings surviving. Another 'Adelante' waits for its next turn of duty on what remains of the shed yard, while the main holding sidings are now on the other side of the main line, on land once occupied by the LNWR/LMS line to Bletchley. The trackbed of the latter can be seen to the left, now in place as an access roadway. Otherwise, trees have grown apace since the 'past' view and, more recently, new housing has appeared on the site of the old shed yard on the right. *Geoff King/MJS*

OXFORD NORTH JUNCTION: Again seen from Walton Well Road bridge, the 'old order' rules but in a slightly amended form! With passenger services withdrawn from Rewley Road from 2 October 1951, services to Bletchley were re-routed to and from the ex-GWR station in Oxford, and this is what is seen here. With the original route into the LNWR/LMS site visible beyond the fourth coach, No 62571 has been forced to cross and, therefore, inconvenience the up main lines, blocking a patiently waiting freight train on a dull and misty 19 March 1952. No 62571 is part way through a long stint as a Cambridge engine. It moved to Lincoln on 20 April 1957, from where the end came on 17 January 1959. The somewhat inconvenient link between the GWR and LMS routes lasted until 29 October 1973. Note St Barnabas's tower again on the horizon.

By 17 July 2005 the whole picture is dramatically changed. The non-navigable link between river and canal remains, but now partly colonised by water plants, the former GWR bridges and tracks over it remain, but elsewhere the view is very different. To the left Oxford is hidden by tree growth and telegraph poles and wires have gone, while to the right new housing and a park area now dominate what was previously the shed yard area. The old trackbed is now a roadway to and from the relatively newly developed 'Turbo' holding sidings. *Alec Ford, MJS collection/ MJS*

OXFORD NORTH JUNCTION: Swinging through 180 degrees, a respectably clean No 7002 *Devizes Castle*, proudly displaying the second British Railways logo on its tender, heads for Oxford with an up parcels train on 23 May 1963, with the main lines in the centre. The still extant ex-LNWR/LMS tracks on the right are now solely dedicated to freight operations into the Rewley Road site. No 7002 was a long-time resident of South Wales, especially around and west of Swansea, but had travelled east on 26 February 1959 with a transfer to Worcester shed. It was withdrawn from there a little over 12 months after this view, on 13 April 1964.

The ex-GWR route is extant, with all four tracks, although the two loops are in less constant use than previously; evidence of this can be judged from the insidious appearance of grass on the up line being taken by No 7002 above. The path of the old route to Bletchley can just be seen to the right, but the view to and across that alignment is largely hidden by bush and tree growth. Note also that new housing now covers the previously open vista, such is the demand for accommodation in this ever-popular city. The 'spindly' bridge taking Aristotle Lane over the railway is a feature common to both views in the extreme upper left. *Geoff King/MJS*

PORT MEADOW HALT: Immediately north of the previously mentioned Aristotle Lane bridge was the diminutive Port Meadow Halt on the Bletchley-Oxford route. With allotments under cultivation across the tracks – accessed by a foot crossing over all the GWR and LNWR tracks – 2-4-0 'Precedent' No 1668 *Dagmar* pauses at the halt shortly after its opening on 9 October 1905. Named Summertown until 1907, to recognise the proximity of this area of Oxford, it closed on 1 January 1917, re-opened on 5 May 1919, then finally shut on 30 October 1926. Built in March 1868, *Dagmar* lasted until 1932, by which time it had been renumbered by the LMS as 5023.

We are now down on the accommodation crossing, still looking north, as ex-LNWR 0-8-0 No 9297 approaches the site of the halt on 6 May 1942 with a rake of War Department empties, presumably from the military site at Bicester Camp. By this time the platform had long gone and an up siding installed, seen just to the left of the train. Interestingly, 'up' here referred to the route to London via Bletchley, so at this point it was running in the opposite direction from the GWR 'up' line on the left! The 0-8-0 was another casualty of withdrawal prior to Nationalisation in 1948. *Peter Treloar collection/A. W. V. Mace collection, Milepost 92½ Picture Library*

PORT MEADOW HALT: The somewhat precarious nature of the accommodation crossing is well seen in this view, from Aristotle Lane bridge, of local engine No 5012 *Berry Pomeroy Castle* heading for Oxford with an inter-regional express in 1958, during one of its sojourns at Oxford shed. Prior to its move there on 27 December 1952, it had served at Laira depot in Devon and Cardiff Canton in South Wales. A brief spell of a month at Old Oak Common in early 1956 split the stay at Oxford, from where the end came on 21 April 1962. Note how the down goods loop curves away from the main line, interrupted by the course of the stream. Port Meadow signal box, on the Bletchley route, can be seen above the third coach; this closed on 28 August 1960.

Dictated by subsequent tree growth, this view is slightly to the right of the earlier one, but the two main lines and the right-hand loop are still extant. On 17 July 2005 No 165128 accelerates along the up main line as the 2L45 FGWL 1126 Bicester Town-Oxford local service. It has just negotiated the crossover seen behind it, coming off the branch; this arrangement was in place from 1973, when the old LMS route to Bicester and beyond was closed up to this point; the trackbed of that route is hidden behind the trees to the right of the train. Note that the accommodation crossing is still in use and that the long down goods loop has been dispensed with and the boundary of the railway straightened. *Peter Treloar/MJS*

WOLVERCOT JUNCTION: Leaving behind the parting of the ways with the LNWR at Port Meadow, the GWR saw another junction at Wolvercot, half a mile or so to the north. Branching left was the route to Kingham, already seen, then almost immediately, at Yarnton, another divergence, this time to Fairford via Witney. In an undated view from the early 1950s, No 7404 is seen between Wolvercot Junction and Yarnton with the 4.15pm Oxford-Fairford local, but still on the Kingham route as it approaches the stop at Yarnton. The shedplate indicates that the loco is shedded at Oxford, where it stayed until 28 December 1963, when it was somewhat dramatically transferred to the wilds of Swansea East Dock for less than seven months' work before withdrawal! Note the Oxford-Banbury main line to the left. *P. G. Barlow, Peter Treloar collection*

YARNTON: In its heyday, arrivals and departures at Yarnton were controlled by this magnificent signal box, opened on 13 June 1909 and with 51 levers after 1927. Situated between the main running lines and the down loop around the station, it closed on 28 March 1971. Seen in 1960, while admittedly giving great views over the surrounding area, any signalman did not need to suffer from vertigo! *Lens of Sutton collection*

YARNTON: From near the end of the down platform the curve to the left for Witney and Fairford is readily apparent, with the line to Kingham stretching into the distance. On 7 June 1960 No 6924 *Grantley Hall* has been given the task of handling this partially-fitted Class D freight, heading for the main line and Oxford, past the plain but informative station nameboard proclaiming 'Yarnton Junction for the Fairford Line'. A long-time servant of the West Midlands sheds, No 6924 came south to Banbury (1953), then Oxford (21 May 1955). When seen here it was operating from Reading shed, but again returned to Oxford on 22 November 1964, from where it saw out its days on 7 October 1965. The bridge in the far distance carries the Yarnton-Cassington road.

Without the benefit of a station platform to stand on – closed on 18 June 1962 – this view was perforce from ground level, but the far-off road bridge is still visible. Elsewhere, all trace of past sidings and platforms, the signal box and the branch to Fairford has disappeared. Another example of the 'take-over' by 'Adelantes' on this route is seen as No 180105 heads for Oxford as the 1F42 FGWL 1117 Worcester Shrub Hill-Paddington service. Note how the absence of front cowling has revealed the identity of front coach No 50905. With all their lack of past charisma, the units' present-day liveries certainly make for a colourful scene! *David Johnson collection/MJS*

Fairford branch

EYNSHAM was the first station proper on the Fairford branch after leaving Yarnton, opened on 14 November 1861 and originally with a single platform. It served in this state for more than 80 years, until provided with a second platform face (the down side for trains towards Witney) in August 1944. Economically it is doubtful whether this truly made sense, as passenger traffic was never very heavy here and facilities were withdrawn on 18 June 1962, less than two decades later. Freight lasted until 26 April 1965, so this view of a passenger train at the station in the snow of April 1970 can only be an enthusiasts' special – here organised by the LCGB. It had been some time since these crossing gates had been opened!

It seems incredible that this could be the same spot, but indeed it is! The B4449 to Stanton Harcourt and Standlake has seen much growth in traffic over the years, which, coupled with the old Yarnton-bound trackbed now being converted to a roadway, to the right, and the old station site now subsumed beneath buildings and an access road for the Oxford Instruments complex, has led to this roundabout. Note, however, that the 'Station Road' sign on the extreme right of this view can still summon memories. The 1944 platform – seen on the extreme left above – was dismantled in 1984 by the Great Western Society and now sees a somewhat more assured life at the Didcot Railway Centre. *John Spencer Gilks/MJS*

EYNSHAM: This slightly straighter view of the approach to Eynsham station on 1 May 1956 shows how much narrower was the B4449 in those days. Looking towards Fairford, the lorry waits for the passage of the train from which this view was taken. A diminutive signal box sits squat on the up platform, while beyond is the more massive goods shed. Surviving for more than two decades after closure in 1965, it was in use for many years as a home for theatre set builders until its demolition in 1987.

That roundabout and the Oxford Instruments building beyond are seen again. Ensuring that he preserved life and limb, your photographer stood just off the roadway built on the old trackbed, but ensured that the shallow embankment, also present on the left in the view above, was retained in the picture. To even the tutored eye, it is hard to visualise a railway ever having been here; apart from the 'Station Road' sign already seen, there is only the merest hint of the former presence in the level and straight alignment of the road. *H. C. Casserley/MJS*

SOUTH LEIGH: Unlike so many stations on our old railway system, South Leigh was actually on the edge of the community it served, but sadly the number of inhabitants was decidedly limited and the roads reaching the tiny village were narrow and full of twists. Opened on 14 November 1861, together with others on the route, the station was ever just a single platform, with a near-square squat wooden building thereon. Opened by the Witney Railway Company, it was not surprising that this building mirrored that provided at the original terminus at Witney, the next station along the route. The angle of this view, taken in August 1965, shows the limited width of the approach road, which formed a T-junction with the road ahead beyond the cars; the 'stalk' of the T swings left over the level crossing at the Oxford end of the station. No 9773 is hauling an LCGB special back from Witney, watched at the crossing gates by a handful of local spectators. The pitched roof seen above the cars belonged to a Second World War food store, served from a siding at the far end of the station.

Even the brooding clouds conspire to echo those above in this comparative view from 40 years later, on 14 July 2005! Changes in traffic levels and Health & Safety considerations are evidenced by the installation of 30mph speed limit signs and road markings guarding the road from the village, to the left. Even on the ground, let alone from this angle, it is hard to discern that a railway once ran here, the sole exception being the still extant station house, called 'Old Crossing'! Two of the old telegraph poles, associated with the railway, have also disappeared. *John Spencer Gilks/ MJS*

WITNEY's original terminus was a single-platform affair, but the attendant yard had plenty of space and accommodation for freight traffic. Opened on 14 November 1861, it closed to passengers a little over a decade later, on 15 January 1873, when the East Gloucestershire Company opened a new station in connection with an extension of the line to Fairford. This is the view in April 1970, during an LCGB enthusiasts' visit. Though some of the buildings still stood into the 1990s, turned to various industrial uses, the station building itself was dismantled and transported to Wallingford for use by the nascent Cholsey & Wallingford Railway preservation group.

The second, closer, view shows the original station building in typical Witney Railway Company style. As can be seen, long after the passenger traffic transferred to the new station the original was still in use for freight traffic. *John Spencer Gilks/Richard Casserley collection*

WITNEY's second station, opened in 1873. As can be seen from the first view, the main station building provided by the East Gloucestershire Company was vastly different from the original one in the town, far grander and built of stone rather than the earlier wooden edifice. This undated view, probably from the late 1950s, is looking towards Fairford and shows the station peaceful between the hustle and bustle associated with the arrival of trains.

The second photograph, from around 1961, shows the view from the A415 Witney-Abingdon road, carried by the bridge seen above. Closed on 18 June 1962, the station only has around another year to serve the locals, but, with the amount of goods items on the platform – including 'Witney' blankets on the trolley – appearances would seem to indicate a healthy state of affairs.

The third view is dated 8 August 1961 and the station is busy, less than a year from the end. No 2221 moves alongside the water column for a refill, while its train waits in the up platform, doors wide open to welcome patronage, before setting off for Oxford. Note the small waiting shelter on the down platform, compared to the far more opulent main building already seen. *MJS collection (2)/Tony Wright*

WITNEY: For our last look at the station, we can enjoy a delightful scene in June 1962 – quite possibly the last day, in view of the number of bodies on the platform. Oxford-based No 9654 waits in the platform while the crew take time out on the left, young and old soak up the atmosphere, and the young boy in the centre proudly holds his camera, presumably having taken his shot of the loco and train. One wonders what ever happened to that photograph! *Paul Chancellor*

BAMPTON, originally 'Bampton (Oxon)' from opening in 1873, became 'Brize Norton & Bampton' on 1 May 1940. Even before this change, brought about due to Second World War demands and the increasing importance of the adjacent Brize Norton airfield, the station was fitted out with a full range of facilities, including livestock, horse boxes and 'carriages and motor cars by passenger train', and even had a 1ton 10cwt crane. Initially with short platforms, these were lengthened in 1940. The first view, from 1 May 1956, looking towards Fairford, shows the extensions together with the main station buildings, signal box, goods shed and sidings. Much of the traffic obviously came from the camp, here to the right.

One year later, on 4 May 1957, the view is from track level and now looking back towards Witney and Oxford. The extension of the down platform on the right can be judged from the difference in the brickwork and the addition of the substantial brick-built signal box. Note the sharp turnout from the up platform to negotiate passage under the Brize Norton-Bampton road bridge. With industrial developments having progressed over time at this site, the only view is from this bridge, and a shot from there is seen in *British Railway Past & Present No 15*, page 99; in 2005 the view would be even more meaningless than when Laurence Waters captured it in 1992!
H. C. Casserley/Richard Casserley

CARTERTON: In 2005 Brize Norton airbase and the village of Carterton are to all intents and purposes one conglomeration, with no discernible break between them. Obviously things have changed since the railway was originally built in 1873, as, heading westwards, the next halt was designated 'Carterton'. The halt was built in 1944 where the line passed beneath a road from Black Bourton to Carterton, to deal with an increase in military traffic – the camp has subsequently subsumed this avenue. With the halt being actually closer to Alvescot – which had its own station – it is little wonder that it was not one of the most used stations on the route after the increase in road traffic to the RAF facility. On 8 August 1961 No 9654 restarts its Fairford-Oxford train away from Carterton, while on the left No 7445 waits to do some shunting, presumably for the camp. Passenger services were withdrawn from 18 June 1962, the same day as the whole stretch from Witney to Fairford closed to all traffic.

With the 'past' view now prevented by the proliferation of tree growth over the succeeding 44 years, this was the closest view possible on 14 July 2005, showing the trackbed, still in obvious regular use by the local farmer, again looking towards Fairford. What was once a pleasant rural railway could now be a pleasant walk! *Tony Wright/MJS*

ALVESCOT, as previously mentioned, was the next station along the branch, only a mile or so from Carterton and situated on the Alvescot-Clanfield road. Note how the typical East Gloucestershire Railway station building, in common with its contemporaries on the route west of Witney, has here been joined by a typical GWR 'pagoda' waiting room. On 2 February 1957, in inclement winter weather, No 2236 arrives with a goods train from Fairford. One of the station staff walks to meet the arrival, which presumably will shunt to add traffic from the coal siding seen in the distance. An Oxford loco at this time, post-Nationalisation saw No 2236 work in South Wales, Somerset, Chester, Shrewsbury, Cardiff and Mid-Wales! It was withdrawn from Machynlleth on 13 June 1965.

Once more moving slightly to obtain a meaningful view – this time to the right – the station house still stands, called, not surprisingly, 'Station Bungalow', and the line of the platform is still there, with a deteriorating wooden fence atop it. As seen on 14 July 2005, coal merchant G. F. Luckett now occupies the trackbed, which continues on its way towards Fairford past the white domed structure in the distance. *Richard Casserley/MJS*

KELMSCOTT & LANGFORD provides our final view on the stretch of the East Gloucestershire Railway within the Oxfordshire county boundary. The halt was in the middle of nowhere, alongside the minor Little Clanfield-Langford road, but was much closer to the latter, with Kelmscott some considerable distance away! Not for the first time, also, the spelling of the station name was slightly different from that of the village of Kelmscot. As seen again on 2 February 1957, looking towards Fairford, the station is graced by a GWR 'pagoda'-type building, rather than the by now familiar and more substantial EGR structures. A single-platform affair, a very short siding was provided at the Fairford end, with a box van just visible there.

With the comparative view once more inaccessible and/or meaningless, this is the scene from the road overbridge on 14 July 2005. The trackbed can be seen heading south-westwards on its way to the county boundary just before Lechlade, with all other evidence of the railway having been swept away by the farmer, with the exception of the pole once holding the station lighting common to both views, but latterly only just visible above the bush! The station access road, entering just left of the farm implement, has been well utilised by the farmer. *Richard Casserley/MJS*

West of England main line: Shrivenham to Steventon and the Faringdon branch

SHRIVENHAM was the most westerly station within the county boundary on the GWR main line out of Paddington. Once an active station, serving not only the local village but also, during the 20th century, the military college on the edge of Shrivenham and the nearby village of Bourton, it had a twin-siding loading/unloading area on the up side serving the college during the war years. The station also boasted long platforms, to accommodate stopping trains, and some of this length, together with the platform loops, is seen in this view of No 2847 heading east with an up mixed freight on 15 August 1954. To the right of the engine is the rather drab-looking Victoria public house.

Fifty years later the scene is rather different! Once more tree growth has dictated an altered vantage point, this time from the Ashbury-Shrivenham road overbridge. On 21 July 2005 No 43030, in the latest incarnation of First Great Western livery, heads east with the 1A11 FGW 0930 Bristol Temple Meads-Paddington express. Note how The Victoria Tavern has been both extended and externally refurbished and now presents a far more appealing prospect. The long platforms remain and there have been regular calls for the station to re-open, possibly as a Swindon Parkway. *Norman Simmons, Hugh Davies collection/MJS*

UFFINGTON: One of the celebrated branch lines within the county was that from Uffington to Faringdon. Admittedly in Berkshire during its life, the locality came into our area with the 1974 county boundary changes. The branch line curved sharply away northwards from the man line at Uffington and this curve can be seen here, with the station and main line to the right. On 26 April 1959 No 1365 runs forward past the signal to couple to the waiting coaches, before heading up the branch with an ex-Swindon REC special. Note the large water tank, serving both main-line and branch locos. Arriving at Swindon from Laira shed on 23 April 1955, No 1365 then stayed there until withdrawal on 9 February 1963.

The fencing on the right gives the game way as to the location and course of the old trackbed, while the old public house that once served the station, seen on the extreme right in the 'past' view, is still there, now occupied as a private residence. The old Station Master's house, off the picture to the right, also still stands, again privately

occupied. On the ground, with the main-line tracks just visible to the right, it is hard to visualise how such a large junction station could have fitted into the available land.
John Spencer Gilks/MJS

94

FARINGDON: We have now joined the special of 26 April 1959 and have travelled the short 3½-mile branch to Faringdon. No 1365 has again run round its train and here stands waiting for the return run down the branch and out on to the main line as the 4pm 'non-stop' to Challow! Opened on 1 June 1864, early thoughts were to continue the run to Lechlade, where it would have made connection with the EGR route to Fairford and would have given the railway to and from Faringdon extra traffic. This did not materialise, however, and after the initial prosperity of the line from the abundance of freight traffic that was handled by the market town, road haulage and buses siphoned business away, with the result that passenger services ceased on 31 December 1951 and freight on 1 July 1963. With human traffic having been absent from the line for more than seven years before this view, it is no wonder that the very young children on the left are fascinated!

The vast majority of the railway's route from the terminus at Faringdon to the outskirts of the town is now lost under various industrial units, but thankfully the station itself has, miraculously, survived. It has been home to varying trades over the years, but in 2005 was a location for a child-minding service! The rooftops and chimney peer over the extension and fencing – as they did above the train in 1959! – and the houses along Park Road give another fix for the location. Many of the long-term residents dearly wish that they could turn back the clock and regain the branch line, especially with recent growth in road traffic along the A420 into Swindon! *John Spencer Gilks/MJS*

96

Opposite page FARINGDON: One of the undoubted highlights of the branch was the design of the terminus at Faringdon. Like 'back-to-back mushrooms', the twin-pitched roof and the tall chimneys gave the structure real aesthetic appeal! As seen in the late 1950s, this is the view from the approach off Park Road. The single passenger platform is on the right, while some of the fairly extensive goods yard can be seen to the left. Just to the left of the tree on the right sat a single-road stone-built engine shed; this was opened by the Faringdon Railway with the branch on 1 June 1864 and included a water tank and coal stage. After closure at the end of 1951, it was let for private use and lasted until the 1970s.

As seen on 24 July 2005, the now listed station building is 'alive and well', occupied by the children's nursery, with an appropriate 'No Parking. Drop off point only' sign. The extension, built some years ago to be in use as a builder's merchant's base, has been carefully added to partly blend in with the original architecture, and only one chimney has disappeared. Happily, in 2005, the platform is still in situ, being utilised within the overall building. *Joe Moss collection, Roger Carpenter collection/MJS*

FARINGDON: I make no excuses for including a further picture of the station complex. Captured during a tour of the town by a local photographer in 1953, the yard is shunted by an unidentified ex-GWR pannier tank, on a trip working from Swindon. Other wagons and box vans from the train stand in the platform awaiting collection. The peak of the engine shed – now converted to other use – can just be seen beyond the wagon, centre left, with the goods shed to the right. Cattle pens are hidden by the loco. It is a scene full of activity, marred only by the knowledge that passenger trains have already ceased. Faringdon had been a prosperous town of some 3,700 souls at the time of the railway arriving, but this had shrunk to 2,900 by the turn of the 20th century and had still not climbed back to the earlier figure by the 1960s! Fifty years after this view, the town still struggles to come to terms with changing fashions and to regain something of its former glory. *Ray Hutt, MJS collection*

UFFINGTON: Back on the main line, we see No 2887 working hard through the station with a down fitted express freight on 15 August 1954. Unlike so many other much smaller stations – and bearing in mind its importance as the junction for Faringdon – Uffington was not graced with a complete set of facilities, with only horse boxes being catered for in addition to the run-of-the-mill passenger and freight duties. Midway along this nearside platform, at the far end of the buildings, was the 47-lever signal box, which closed on 3 March 1968. To the right is the old Junction Hotel, advertising 'Cab for Hire'. A Severn Tunnel Junction loco at the date of this photograph, No 2887 was truly a South Wales engine until 28 September 1963, when it went to Reading. A transfer to Taunton came on 28 December of the same year, from where it was withdrawn on 20 July the following year.

At full line speed of 125mph, an unidentified HST roars past the old station site, with most passengers on the 1C22 FGW 1000 Paddington-Bristol Temple Meads service probably blissfully unaware of the location they are briefly visiting. Note that the Junction Hotel is still in situ, but now very much a private residence, yet still complete with the shed on site in 1954! Elsewhere in this view there is no evidence of the old station. *Norman Simmons, Hugh Davies* collection/MJS

CHALLOW was the next station eastwards. Situated by the A417 main road between Faringdon and Wantage, two of the major towns in the area, it was opened on 20 July 1840 as Faringdon Road, originally just a 'normal' station with double track and two platform faces. Development by the GWR in 1933 saw four tracks through the station, with new, longer platforms and the widening of the road bridge span. Passenger numbers were at their height in the post-First World War years, with a gradual decline thereafter, and, together with others on the route, it closed on 7 December 1964. The first view from 4 May 1957, looking east towards Didcot, shows the footbridge and functional but not displeasing station building.

Having been taken out of use in 1965, the two loops lines were quickly taken up and the station buildings and footbridge removed, leaving the scene as here, with just denuded platforms remaining on either side of the main line. On 24 August 1989 'celebrity' Class 37 No 37350 – the former pioneer English Electric Type 3 D6700 – in its recreation of the original livery, double-heads No 37215 through the station site with the 1120 Theale-Robeston oil tanks.

Since then there has been progress both positive and negative! Through 1992/3 the platforms at Challow were removed, to allow space for new loop lines – though why the original alignments could not have been utilised, thus allowing for even the slim possibility of re-opening the station, is a mystery! The positive feature, however, was the re-instatement of quadruple tracks, which gave extra capacity and enabled more trains to use the route and therefore justify the services and give greater hope for the future. On 21 July 2005 No 43143 – named *Stroud 700* at Stroud station on 15 April 2004 – brings up the rear of an up express as it roars through the station approaching 125mph. *Richard Casserley/MJS (2)*

CHALLOW: Here is one final view of No 1365 with the REC special previously seen at Faringdon on 26 April 1959. Here it has arrived (at 4.18pm precisely!) with the 4pm non-stop run from Faringdon, has disgorged its complement of passengers, and is slowly propelling its two-coach stock backwards, before running round and continuing on to Swindon as empty stock. Tour participants take a last look at their train, presumably well aware of the significance of their recent experience. Note the large goods shed in the background, with its doorway unusually spanning two tracks. Although closed on 7 December 1964, goods traffic managed to struggle on until the following 29 March.

With platforms, signal box, goods shed, etc all gone, the site has now become just another lineside view, devoid of previous attraction. On 21 July 2005 an unidentified HST power car shows wisps of exhaust as it accelerates through Challow on its way towards Swindon, as the 1B22 FGW 1015 Paddington-Cardiff Central service. With odd rails lying around and clean ballast on and between the two up lines, there has obviously been some recent engineering work here. *David Lawrence, Hugh Davies collection/MJS*

WANTAGE ROAD station, opened on 1 June 1840, was some 2 miles from the town it purported to serve, but at least there was later a link between the two by way of the Wantage Tramway. Initially built as twin-track, as seen here in 1919, with rudimentary waiting shelters, transformation of the station came in 1932, when the GWR refashioned the up side – most prominent in this view looking towards Didcot – by sweeping away the original platform, widening the trackbed to quadruple the lines and providing a fresh down platform on the southern side of the line. In front of the large Pears' Soap advert the station is liberally supplied with milk churns, but this was a time of maximum business here, with a decline setting in around the mid-1920s. Note the three-storey main station building perched atop the embankment at the side of the A338 Wantage-Oxford road.

Yet another HST roars its way west on 21 July 2005, this time forming the 1B25 FGW 1045 Paddington-Swansea express. The original brick A338 road bridge has been replaced by a stronger version – which saw remedial action during the summer of 2005, shortly after this view – and the footbridge, which partly masks the 'past' view, and the rest of the station furniture have all gone. The up platform remains on this side, together with part of the down one. A length of the latter, closer to the road bridge, was removed when new loops were installed in 1992/3. As with Shrivenham, there have been many calls for this station to re-open, especially with the increasing road congestion locally and the growth in population in both Wantage and nearby Grove.
Richard Casserley collection/MJS

STEVENTON: This is an unexceptional picture, yet one that highlights yet another wayside station that served its local population well and which, this time, was right on its doorstep. Steventon station was, from 1 June until 20 July 1840, the terminus of the expanding GWR, and the railhead for traffic to and from Oxford for four years, until the city had its own station. Such was its brief importance that an impressive structure was provided as the Station Superintendent's house, and was used for GWR company board meetings between July 1842 and January 1843! In this view, looking east towards Didcot on 13 March 1957, the station has settled into its latterly mundane existence, before it closed to passengers on 7 December 1964, although freight continued until May of the following year. Loop lines began immediately after the original A34 Abingdon-Newbury road bridge.

Not a strict comparison, due to the intrusion of the engineering train on the down line, but this is the same place, with the previous platform area to the left of the road/rail machine on this nearside up track. On 19 February 2005 work is under way on track renewal, a feature of the railway that many of the public neither appreciate nor fully understand. No 66210, one of the now ubiquitous EWS Class 66 freight locomotives, stands ready to move forward with its train of new sleepers. *Richard Casserley/MJS*

STEVENTON: 'Duke' Class 4-4-0 *Isle of Jersey* leaves Steventon on a Swindon-Paddington train in this undated view. The station is just visible on the other side of the A34 bridge, and the tall chimneys of that grandiose Superintendent's house can just be seen above the right-hand edge of the road bridge.

During that same engineer's possession of the main line on 19 February 2005, a tractor indulges in some ballast levelling, standing in roughly the same position as *Isle of Jersey*. The road bridge is still in situ, but the A34 has now become a major trunk road and has been re-routed away from the village, leaving this road to take people either into Didcot or on to the new A34 dual carriageway. Note that the loops are still in existence but now no longer come this close to the bridge, and that there has been new palisade fencing installed on the far side.
Richard Casserley collection/MJS

South from Oxford

HINKSEY YARD: Moving back to immediately south of Oxford station, we are treated to a truly wonderful and remarkable shot of the down side of Hinksey yard in 1958. To say that the site is busy is to put it mildly, and as well as showing just how much of our national freight has been lost overall from the railway, it is a superb example of the intricacies of yard management. Imagine trying to programme what is to go where, when and, perhaps most importantly, how! With the Hinksey Stream to the right, No 3857 rests with its relatively short rake of mixed vans and wagons before restarting its journey north with its headcode designating 'pick-up freight'. Here proudly displaying its 81F (Oxford) shed code on the smokebox, it moved to Severn Tunnel Junction shed in 1960, then Banbury in 1962, before being withdrawn from that shed on 13 April 1964. *Peter Treloar*

Opposite page HINKSEY YARD: The southern half of the yard is here seen from Abingdon Road bridge on 17 August 1963, with No 7824 *Iford Manor* accelerating from the Oxford stop on the 10.30am Birmingham (Snow Hill)-Hastings inter-regional service and displaying an unhealthy burst of black smoke! Beyond the third coach stands the 72-lever Hinksey South signal box, opened in wartime on 29 March 1942 and lasting until 18 December 1973, when the power box on Oxford station took control of the yard and its environs. Note the narrow throat to the yard, with access from just the main down line and, on the left, a long loop.

A little over 42 years later Hinksey yard is still in active service, but the entrance and subsequent layout within the yard have seen much change over the years. The long loop and the main-line link still give access, but thereafter much has changed. With the proposed introduction of a 'virtual quarry' at the northern end of the yard, track on site was dramatically remodelled during 2001, with the increased number and length of sidings officially opening on 11 July. These lie beyond No 66130, which is seen crawling its way from the yard before accelerating along the loop beneath us. On the main line on 20 July 2005, No 166220 gathers speed with the 2P40 FGWL 0936 Banbury-Paddington service. Note the track rationalisation and spread of greenery since the earlier view. *Edwin Wilmshurst/MJS*

HINKSEY YARD: A rather fuller view of Hinksey Stream is seen on the right in this view looking south from Abingdon Road bridge. On 10 July 1965 No 6126 brings a local freight from Didcot along the long loop line that will take it into Hinksey Yard. The A423 dual carriageway Ring Road crosses on the bridge in the distance. An Oxford loco at the time, since 19 May 1964, it lasted just another six months after this view, being withdrawn on 15 January 1966, consequent on the closure to steam of Oxford shed.

The ever-increasing growth of trees and bushes seen elsewhere in this volume is graphically demonstrated in this comparative view from 20 July 2005. The Stream still wends its way, this time looking slightly healthier than 40 years earlier, but the view to the railway is now severely restricted. Note also how the trees on the right appear to have arrived from nowhere compared with 1965. An unidentified Thames 'Turbo' heads for Oxford forming a local service from Didcot. The A423 Ring Road bridge is still there, but now hidden by the trees. *Edwin Wilmshurst/MJS*

RADLEY: Accessed from a minor road running south from Kennington, on the southern outskirts of Oxford, and parallel to the main A34 to Abingdon, Radley was the next major station stop on the route from Oxford to Didcot. As well as serving the local community, it was also the junction for the branch to Abingdon, and in this 10 August 1963 view a DMU stands in the branch platform on the extreme left. Looking towards Oxford, with the nearby village further to the left (although the main road access was from the right!), both platforms have more than adequate waiting accommodation, with a covered footbridge joining them. As with other locations we have seen, the 41-lever signal box was located on the platform. It closed on 21 May 1965, and the cast-iron running-in board was subsequently moved to the NRM in York. Happily, the station has not suffered the indignity of having passenger services withdrawn, although the Abingdon branch passenger traffic was lost from 9 September 1963 and it lost its freight facilities in the goods yard alongside the branch platform on 27 June 1971.

Under a threatening sky, Virgin 'Voyager' No 220010 *Ribble Voyager* (named at Preston on 26 March 2002) heads south through the station, watched by a solitary young lady. The footbridge remains, now with no outward sign of GWR origins, but otherwise the unmanned station is now a very bare shadow of its former self. Note that the branch platform is still in situ, but that the track for this and the adjacent goods yard has all gone, removed in 1973, leaving the space to be filled by the inevitable car park. *Paul Chancellor collection/MJS*

ABINGDON station frontage, at the end of the branch from Radley, was simple and understated, yet delightfully attractive. Built in 1908 after the original structure was demolished after being damaged in a shunting accident on 22 April, the new version – without its original 'GWR' above the lettering – is viewed from the appropriately named Station Road around 1963. It was finally swept away in 1971, some time after passenger services were withdrawn on 9 September 1963. A large malthouse can be seen to the left.

Taken from close to the same spot on 30 July 2005, this is now the view, following the construction of a Waitrose supermarket. The closest link to the above is the line of the passage down the left-hand side of both station and supermarket. The housing development on the left refers in its name to the old malthouse. *Paul Chancellor collection/MJS*

ABINGDON: We have now moved through the station building to the single platform, looking back towards the vantage point of the page opposite. A double-decker bus waits for custom in Station Road, with, to the right, the chimneys of the Railway public house and the low roof of a builder's merchant's site. Seen around 1962 a single-car DMU apparently in ex-works condition, with appropriate destination blind, is all that is required for the branch traffic, so close to the end of passenger services. Some items of the still healthy freight traffic at the time can be seen to the left. Note the squat solitary lamp on the platform.

The Waitrose supermarket is seen again, but from the opposite end, showing the delivery area in the centre, the passage on the right, and the main car park to the left. Another aspect of the 'malthouse' housing development can be seen on the extreme right. *MJS collection/MJS*

CULHAM: With a freight train disappearing into the distance, its locomotive producing a clean exhaust, No 6923 *Croxteth Hall* enters Culham station, the next stop south from Radley, on 9 May 1964. It is hauling a York-Bournemouth cross-country service, consisting of a rake of SR green-liveried coaches. Opened on 12 June 1844 and named 'Abingdon Road' until 1856, Culham was and is some considerable distance from the village after which it is named, but had the advantage for many years of having the Royal Navy Air Station nearby. The goods shed, closed with the yard on 19 July 1965, is prominent on the left, while to the right we can just glimpse the 29-lever signal box, rebuilt in 1952 but closed on 12 February 1961. A caravan sits incongruously on the cattle pen platform.

The basic platform layout survives, but on 30 July 2005 a new variant has been introduced. Concurrently with

the introduction of one-man-operated Thames 'Turbos' in the early 1990s came a rethink of the use of the station and the provision of passenger facilities on the up platform. The old one was closed and a completely new one opened at the Oxford end; the slope of the latter and its waiting shelter are seen to the right of No 180112, running non-stop through the station as the 1F34 FGWL 0910 Worcester Shrub Hill-Paddington service. The goods shed and all sidings have been removed, leaving the site much diminished in interest, but the aesthetics have been improved by the growth of trees, the well-kept platforms and the smart paintwork. *Bryan Hicks/MJS*

CULHAM: In late-Victorian times the position of the goods shed was merely a short bay platform. Looking towards Didcot, note the ivy-covered signal box on the left, the crossover from the up line to the goods siding and the wide dock platform, with access via the Railway Hotel, seen in the right background. The station displays the delightful Brunel chalet-type design that was once far more common than in later years. Note that passengers were forced to cross between platforms by the barrow crossing at the platform ends.

An almost exact comparison from 9 June 1959 shows that the down platform has been substantially lengthened, resulting in the loss of the previous short dock. The siting of the signal box has also changed, with the 1952 rebuild now on the platform, rather than off the end of it. A rather grand footbridge has also been provided, complete with overall roof, but elsewhere the platform buildings are as before, with the addition of seating for some travelling comfort.

On 30 July 2005 the current layout clearly shows the past and the present. The old up platform is as before, as are the chalet station building – which enjoyed major refurbishment during 2004 – and the footbridge, although without its roof. The Railway Hotel is still serving thirsty customers and the road overbridge remains, but is now in limited use, following the opening of a bypass some years ago. The new up platform is on the left, and this must be one of very few sites in the UK with two platforms 'nose-to-nose' in this fashion, especially when one is not in use! Sadly, seating has been removed from the down platform.
MJS collection/Richard Casserley/ MJS

APPLEFORD is seen here, looking north on 1 January 1981. Designated a 'Halt' until 5 May 1969, it was very different in nature from both its neighbours at Culham and Radley, being very much more a small wayside station, with 'pagoda' waiting shelters and very little else in the way of passenger facilities, due to an opening date as late as 11 September 1933. Also, the station has wooden platforms and is restricted by not having a purpose-built parking/waiting area. For many years, by the side of the steps seen leading to the up platform on the right, there was a sign that advised potential travellers that 'Railway tickets may be obtained at the Post Office'!

Twenty-four years later, on 30 July 2005, relatively little has changed, with replacement access stairs, lighting and waiting shelters the main features. It is still a wayside halt, but the platform surface is now more reassuring compared to the previous wooden structure! *Colin Caddy/MJS*

Didcot

DIDCOT station was opened on 12 June 1844 with the simultaneous opening of the line to Oxford. The track was on a higher level than the surrounding station area, so the platforms were accessed from below, as can be seen in this view from 1 January 1981. To the right stands the massive former Station Master's house, now partly transformed into a Travel Centre, with the main body of the public side beyond. Note the buffer stop, centre left, at the end of a short siding. The notice in the hedge to the left of the bike shed states 'No Parking', indicating that the area in front was for buses. Several potential passengers approach in the late afternoon sunshine.

The transformation has been both dramatic and complete in this view of the same location on 30 July 2005. With increasing demands made on the old station into the 1980s, it was time for a rethink and rebuild, and the new structure, now known as Didcot Parkway, was opened on 29 July 1985. With a far more modern appearance and more spacious entrance/ticket area, the station still looks presentable, especially with the 'First' logo, but the wooden pitched roof looks as though it could do with some attention, 20 years after it was built. The previous short siding with the buffer stop has long been swept away and is now subsumed within an alternative exit from the main down platform and car park area. *Colin Caddy/MJS*

DIDCOT: The previously mentioned short siding can be seen to the right of this view of the down main platform on 14 September 1974, although the box van is somewhat isolated as the tracks have been taken up! No 47467 is arriving at Platform 1 with a Paddington-Swansea service, with impending travellers patiently waiting. The station canopies are virtually unaltered since construction in 1892, surviving the 1932 lengthening and straightening of the platforms, with only the tops of the lift shafts now prominent. No 47467 was built in June 1964 and spent much of its life operating from South Wales depots, but was ousted from front-line passenger services by the introduction of HSTs on the former GWR lines from 1975. Thereafter it was more widely travelled, finally being withdrawn from Immingham on 12 December 1998.

Yet more patient travellers wait on Platform 1 on 30 July 2005. Once more there has been both much and little change! The canopies of the up platforms are largely as before, but on the down platform, subsequent to the 1985 rebuilding of the entrance hall, they have gone, and the sheltered waiting area on the platform has been shortened. The fencing on the right still remains, but the area beyond it is now greatly altered, with cars now parked right up to the platform edge. No 43024 slows for the stop as the 1C29 FGW 1130 Paddington-Weston-super-Mare service. *Tom Heavyside/MJS*

DIDCOT: The first photograph was used in *British Railways Past & Present No 15*, but I make no excuses for repetition as it fits nicely with the two shots below. The road straight ahead is to Swindon, while the right-hand curve is to Oxford and was formally known as Chester Line Junction, recognising that trains taking that route were ultimately heading in the direction of the most northerly outpost of the GWR empire! The scene, including the saddle-tank shunting a rake of wagons and the large Provender Store in the background, is from 25 July 1919.

The comparative view from 18 July 1963 shows the alterations wrought by the 1932 platform lengthening and track realignments. The 1884 Provender Store and Didcot West End signal box – replacing the earlier one of that name seen above – provide a link between the two views, but the alterations to both platforms and track layout can clearly be seen. No 4929 *Goytrey Hall*, a Gloucester (Horton Road) engine for the whole of its British Railways life, passes behind the signal box at the head of an up empty engineer's train that has originated many, many miles away at Marazion. The loco was withdrawn in March 1965.

Yet more change has taken place by 30 July 2005. The right-hand platform face next to No 4929 above is no longer in place and the area has been fenced off. In addition, over the past 42 years the sidings have gone and a large car park constructed in their place. A footbridge now spans the tracks, taking car owners to and from the station, the signal box, Provender Store and adjacent broad/standard gauge transfer shed have all gone, and the horizon is now dominated by the massive cooling towers of Didcot Power Station, completed in 1971. Happily the freight yard, to the right, is still very active. *MJS collection (2)/MJS*

DIDCOT ENGINE SHED: The initial facility here was a two-road affair, situated near to and opened with the station on 12 June 1844. This only lasted until July 1857, however, when it was replaced by a three-road, dead-end structure with a slated gable-style roof. The 1932 station rebuilding required the site for extra tracks, so the four-road brick and corrugated asbestos building that remains today was provided in that year, on an alignment closer to the loop line. It eventually closed to steam on 5 April 1965. Seen here on 27 September 1959, No 5351 occupies a prominent position in the yard, with No 4965 *Rood Ashton Hall* standing outside the shed on the left; they were withdrawn on 17 June 1961 and 24 March 1962 respectively, both from Didcot.

To show just how good the Great Western Society has been at recreating past views, this shot from 5 May 1990 is almost timeless – apart from the presence of the 'Western' diesel on the right. Left to right, we have Nos 5572, 5322 and 6998 *Burton Agnes Hall*, withdrawn in April 1962 (from Laira), April 1964 (from Pontypool Road) and December 1965 (from Oxford) respectively, and all happily rescued from the 'grim reaper'! *Norman Preedy/MJS*

Oxford to Thame

LITTLEMORE: The former branch from Oxford to Thame and Princes Risborough left the Oxford-Didcot line at Kennington Junction, and, apart from a short-lived halt at Iffley, the first station heading east on the branch was at Littlemore, a mile from the junction. Opened on 24 October 1864, it was graced with a full range of passenger and freight provision, including a 3-ton crane and sidings, some of which served over the years National Benzole Co Ltd and Oxford County & City Mental Hospital! This view, taken from the A423 Oxford-Wallingford road on an extremely wet 16 June 1956, shows the mental hospital top right. Looking towards Princes Risborough, the extent of the sidings and goods yard is clear from this angle. The station building was little changed throughout its 98-year life.

After the withdrawal of passenger services between Oxford and Princes Risborough on 6 January 1963, the line remained open until May 1967, but then the middle section from Horspath to Thame was fully closed and lifted. The Oxford end remained open, largely due to traffic to and from the Morris Cowley complex. This traffic still continues, following the take-over by BMW and the more recent success of the new 'Mini'. The route here is now just a single track, with apparently no vestige of the previous station, as seen on 20 July 2005. However, the building remains in situ, swallowed within the A. W. Clarke (Engineering) Ltd complex. Situated immediately behind the flat-topped building just beyond the trees, it even retains its original roof, but in a slightly different position – it was effectively slid to the right, with the slope now in view being the previous platform canopy! The two buildings of the asylum still stand, but now hidden by yet more tree growth. *Richard Casserley/MJS*

MORRIS COWLEY station and factory complex are just over a mile further east. Such have been recent developments that access was virtually impossible during the preparation of this book, and the reader is therefore referred to the earlier *Oxfordshire* volume, where Laurence Waters has an almost identical view and a comparative view from around 1992. Looking back towards Oxford on 14 April 1962, the 1928-vintage station is seen in all its glory, standing on the site of the previous Garsington Bridge Halt, which was in operation between 1 February 1908 and 22 March 1915. As may be judged, it was only honoured with the most rudimentary of passenger and freight facilities, apart from sidings to the car works, but it did enjoy the provision of a 6-ton crane! Some of the sidings are just visible beyond the far end of the platform. One or two parcels await collection/disposal on the platform, while signs denote 'Booking Hall and Waiting Room', 'Ladies Waiting Room' and the 'Gentlemen'.

Walking to the Oxford end of the station on the same day, we see a train about to depart for that city, having come from Princes Risborough behind No 6124. We can see more of the car complex on either side of the station and more sidings immediately to the right of the loco. No 6124 had come to Oxford shed on 27 January 1962, having previously served Slough and Didcot in the 1950s. It moved to Old Oak Common on 4 May 1963, then to South Wales, to Radyr, north of Cardiff, exactly one year later, from where it was withdrawn on 20 July 1964. *Both Edwin Wilmshurst*

WHEATLEY is another location where a 'present' view is either not possible or is meaningless – again the reader is referred to the earlier book for a more enlightening set of comparisons. However, rather than exclude the location altogether, we here have a view in much happier times! On 20 April 1958, with the branch still in full swing, an enthusiasts' tour makes a stop for participants to enjoy the surroundings. No 9017 gently simmers at the head of the REC's 'The Severn Rambler', the 8.45am Windsor Central-Cheltenham (St James) train. Note the goods in the far sidings and the predominance of suits and 'jackets and flannels' for the tour members – a far cry from what would be worn today! A Machynlleth loco for the whole of its British Railways life, the 'Dukedog' had been withdrawn on 8 October 1960, but was saved for preservation by the Bluebell Railway, where it has most times worn its previous GWR number of 3217. *John Spencer Gilks*

119

TIDDINGTON: Once again I point you in the direction of volume No 15 in this series, as the present situation at Tiddington precludes any meaningful shot – even in 1992 it was little better! Thus we can only look back at what once was, which in this instance is an unidentified '61xx' 2-6-2T entering the station with a Princes Risborough-Oxford branch-line train. A diminutive signal box sits on the ground on the right, to control both the passage of trains and also the short cattle dock, the end of which can be seen on the left. A short platform housed the small station building, which, despite its size, looks highly presentable in this undated view, probably from the very early 1960s. The station, which closed on 7 January 1963, could once handle horse boxes as well as livestock, employed a 3-ton crane and had a siding added in 1921 for a Board of Trade timber supply depot.

Looking in the opposite direction, we now look towards Oxford for this view from 29 June 1963. Six months after closure, the once 'pretty' building is now looking decidedly the worse for wear, stripped of poster boards and seat, and with the entrance doorway closed and padlocked. The cattle dock is empty – although the siding remained in use until the end of 1963 – and grass is encroaching on the platform surface, but incredibly there looks to have been some engineering work done in the not too distant past, with concrete sleepers replacing the wooden ones of the earlier view. Note that the station nameboard survives. *MJS collection/P. J. Garland, Roger Carpenter collection*

THAME was by far the most important station on the branch, recognising the importance of this thriving Oxfordshire market town. The twin platforms, together with cattle docks on both sides and additional sidings, demonstrate that importance. Opened by the Wycombe Railway on 2 August 1862, it had, not surprisingly, a full range of passenger and freight facilities, and the yard made use of a 6-ton crane. Seen on 14 April 1962, an Oxford-bound DMU set sits under the delightful Brunel-style overall trainshed. All the sidings on the up side contain goods wagons, and the whole has an air of quiet prosperity. However, the station closed on 7 January 1963, with the goods yard following on 10 October 1966. A large water tower stands on the opposite side of the B4012, but this did not serve the railway as another tank met the station's needs, just out of the picture to the left. We are looking directly towards the heart of the town, beyond the trees in the distance.

Incredibly, despite the abandonment of the site and trackbed after final closure in September 1991 – traffic to an oil terminal just beyond the road bridge had survived until this date – rails still lie in situ in the old cattle dock in the foreground, and the platforms are still extant, with a footpath now occupying the space between. The old goods yard was transformed in the late 1980s by the development of a substantial industrial site. At least no one can be in any doubt that a railway once ran here! *Edwin Wilmshurst/MJS*

Watlington branch

CHINNOR: As well as the GWR main line from London to Birmingham running through the station, Princes Risborough was also a terminus for three branch lines at its height. The most southerly of these was that to Watlington, and other than halts Chinnor was the first station on the line. Initially opened by the Watlington & Princes Risborough Railway on 15 August 1852 in open countryside, a lime-burning site was established nearby in 1908 and was rail linked. This developed into a cement works over the years and was the source of much rail traffic right up until the final train ran on 20 December 1989. Looking towards Princes Risborough, this is the view of the station on 13 September 1958, with the siding from the goods yard on the left. This latter remained open for local traffic until 10 October 1966.

After official closure of the cement works on 16 July 1990, volunteers and supporters of the Chinnor & Princes Risborough Railway Association moved in, with the aim of restoring both station and, ultimately, the line back to Princes Risborough. The station building had gone by this time, giving the enthusiasts another headache. 1998 saw work start on building a replica of the original, and the results can be seen here on 20 July 2005, a lovingly crafted recreation that gives the impression that the original had never disappeared. To accommodate longer trains than of yore, the platform was extended towards the road bridge. The coach stands on the alignment of the old siding seen above. *Richard Casserley/MJS*

ASTON ROWANT: South of Chinnor the railway has been long abandoned and station sites are now no longer recognisable. Thus we feature instead views of the remaining two main stations on the branch, and again readers are referred to the earlier 'Past and Present' volume for something approaching meaningful comparisons. Aston Rowant opened with the rest of the line on 15 August 1872. The station building is obviously from the same template as Chinnor, and, like its near neighbour, it was situated in a very rural setting, some way from any habitation, despite being next to the main A40 trunk road. In this view from 29 June 1957, looking towards the stops at Watlington, the goods siding, serving a shed with its own office, runs in behind the platform on the right. *Edwin Wilmshurst*

<table>
<tr><td>Gt. Western Ry.</td><td></td><td>Gt. Western Ry.</td></tr>
<tr><td colspan="3">Watlington   Watlington</td></tr>
<tr><td colspan="3">TO</td></tr>
<tr><td colspan="3">BLEDLOW BRIDGE HALT</td></tr>
<tr><td colspan="3">THIRD CLASS</td></tr>
<tr><td colspan="3">1/2 C   Fare   1/2 C</td></tr>
<tr><td>Bledlow Bridge</td><td></td><td>Bledlow Bridge</td></tr>
<tr><td colspan="3">FOR CONDITIONS SEE BACK E.B</td></tr>
</table>

WATLINGTON: We have now reached the end of the line at another station situated outside the village it purported to serve. On the same day as above, 29 June 1957, the last day of services, No 4650 enters the station with a single-coach train from Princes Risborough. Note the goods shed to the left and the typically capped water tower behind the train. The last scheduled freight served the goods shed on a cold, wet and miserable 30 December 1960. The two small corrugated huts to the left of the loco were oil stores. No 4650 was a Slough loco at this time – indeed, in latter years, engines for the service ran from Slough at 5.38am each day to be ready for the passenger services! – but was transferred to South Wales on 21 May 1960, from where it ended its working days on 8 August 1965. *Mike Esau*

Wallingford branch

WALLINGFORD: If the course of the Watlington branch had continued beyond the terminus, it would eventually have met up with the railway at Wallingford, the terminus of a short branch opened on 2 July 1866 from Cholsey on the GWR main line from London to Bristol. Wallingford itself was another extremely picturesque GWR branch-line station and some of this charm can be seen in this view towards the buffer stops on 16 August 1947. The main A4130 road from Didcot ran past the station between the buffer stops and the large house seen in the distance. The large 3,000-gallon water tank – a replacement in 1920 for the original – stands in front of the single-road engine shed, while a brake-van stands in the dock road, which had an end-loading platform, seen here with the gate removed. No 1447 stands in the single platform, waiting to earn its keep by running the solitary coach to Cholsey. The brick-built engine shed, dating from 1890, when it replaced the previous wooden version, lasted in BR's hands until February 1956, but then survived well into the mid-1960s in private use. Passenger services ceased on 15 June 1959, with freight following on 13 September 1965, but by this time Associated British Maltsters had established a mill with sidings next to the line in the town and trains to this plant lasted until 1981.

In similar vein to the Chinnor preservation society already seen, volunteers and enthusiasts moved in to salvage what was left before redevelopment after closure of the malt mill took hold. Successfully running their

first train in April 1988, the Cholsey & Wallingford Railway Preservation Society has since developed its own base and managed to acquire parts of the old mill area to extend its sphere of operation. Like so many young societies, the struggle is often hard and long, but they are gaining a well-deserved reputation for what they do. As the original terminus has been lost to another development – again see volume No 15 – this is a comparative view, on 3 July 2005, with the original platform, but taken from nearer the Cholsey end. A train top-and-tailed by ex-BR Class 08s waits to begin the run to Cholsey. *H. C. Casserley/MJS*

CHOLSEY & MOULSFORD was the other end of the branch, and the usual branch train in later years – a single-coach push-pull auto-train – is seen on 14 June 1958, with No 1407 resting in the bay platform before returning to Wallingford as the 3.10pm departure. A run-round loop was provided but rarely used, and the service was withdrawn exactly one year and one day later. On the down relief line on the left, a train for Didcot disappears into the distance. A Reading loco when seen here – that shed operated all trains after the shed at Wallingford was closed – No 1407 moved to Southall on 27 February 1960, from where it was withdrawn on 18 June of the year.

A determined aim from the outset, when the preservationists moved in to Wallingford in 1981, was to regain access by train to Cholsey's bay platform. This was initially achieved in 1994, and continued intermittently over the years, but it was to be 1999 before regular services returned to the branch. While many of the intervening trains had been steam-hauled – and, indeed, this was preferred by the public – the view on 3 July 2005 shows one of the railway's two ex-BR 08s, posing with the crew for their portrait before returning to Wallingford. *John Spencer Gilks/MJS*

Opposite page CHOLSEY & MOULSFORD: The main line seen to the left of the platform on the previous page is here spotlighted, with No 5064 *Bishop's Castle* pausing as the Saturday's-only 2.40pm Reading-Didcot local on 27 September 1958. A Swindon loco, as denoted by its 82C shedplate, and with four years of life left, it would seem to be a rather humble train for this powerful locomotive to be hauling, but, judging by its external condition, it is presumably on a 'running-in' turn after Works attention at Swindon. Having been shedded at Shrewsbury when inherited by British Railways in 1948, a move to Bristol (Bath Road) came on 31 December 1950, before transferring to Swindon on 22 March 1958. Staying there until 7 October 1961, the final move was to Gloucester (Horton Road), from where it was withdrawn on 8 September 1962. Note the full-sized 'Cholsey & Moulsford. Change for Wallingford' station nameboard, and the similarity between the station building and that at Culham.

On a dull 30 July 2005, the clean Thames 'Turbo' does not match up to the appeal of the steam locomotive! No 165117 restarts the 1D25 FGWL 1121 Paddington-Oxford stopper from Cholsey, having collected its complement of waiting passengers. In the far distance Virgin 'Voyager' No 221101 *Louis Bleriot* approaches at speed with an express cross-country service that will overtake this slower train to Didcot. Note the attractive resurfacing of the platform since the earlier view, the erection of new fencing and lighting, and the waiting shelter now without any canopy. Also, the station name signs have been drastically shortened to just 'Cholsey'. *Richard Casserley/MJS*

Our final view is 'past and present' in one picture! The 'present' is the 1995-constructed Wallingford bypass, which could have scuppered the railway's attempts at regaining Cholsey if they had not already managed to extend their operations to that station before the plans for this new road were in their final stages of consideration. It does mean that the railway obviously has to take great care in crossing the road, but thus far this has not been a problem. Over the weekend of 18/19 June 2005, the railway achieved something of a coup when it managed to host a visit by the celebrated *City of Truro*. Seen on the Saturday, the ex-GWR loco, famed for being the first engine to claim 100mph in 1904, here with its 'express passenger' headcode – and with a representative of the Queen on board! – flies the flag for the 'past' as it crosses the bypass at a much gentler speed than a century earlier! Ray Towell, the NRM's representative, waves from the cab. *Cliff Thomas*

INDEX OF LOCATIONS